Wicked FISHERS

Wicked FISHERS

Robert Bowling

THE History PRESS

Published by The History Press
Charleston, SC
www.historypress.com

First published 2021

Manufactured in the United States

ISBN 9781467144629

Library of Congress Control Number: 2021934301

Notice: The information in this book is true and complete to the best of our knowledge. It is offered without guarantee on the part of the author or The History Press. The author and The History Press disclaim all liability in connection with the use of this book.

I dedicate this book to my family.
My wife, Michelle, and our three boys, Bo, Matt and Nate.

CONTENTS

Acknowledgements 9
Introduction 11

1. An Illegal Prize Fight 19
2. The Ghost of James Payne 27
3. The Legend of Heady Hollow 31
4. Fall Creek Indian Massacre 35
5. Junction 69 43
6. The Battle of Mudsock 51
7. A White Cap Beating? 61
8. The Mystery of the Eller Bridge Arson 65
9. The City under the Lake 71
10. The Grave Robbing Trials of 1903 75
11. The Great School Controversy 99
12. The Mysterious Trittipo Bombings 107
13. Turkey Shoot Leads to Murder 115
14. Robbery of the Fishers National Bank 123
15. The Murder of Constable Frank Carey 133
16. The Pharmacist Who Sold More than Drugs 141

Bibliography 145
About the Author 159

ACKNOWLEDGEMENTS

There are two people who deserve particular recognition for their assistance in the writing of this book.

First, David Heighway, the Hamilton County historian, gave me the inspiration to write this book based on some of his previous research. He has always been willing to answer questions and help me with research. We have collaborated together on history projects like the historical reenactment of the Battle of Mudsock, which is discussed in this book. He was instrumental in finding a descendant of Hampton West, who made the trip from North Carolina to Indiana to watch the reenactment. His passion for history encourages me to keep pursing my love for history.

Secondly, I want to acknowledge Larry Reynolds, author of the *Mudsock Scrapbook*. A lifelong resident of Fishers and founder of Reynolds Farm Equipment, he now lives in Florida. His sons continue to run the business. There is perhaps no person who better understands the local history of Fishers than Larry Reynolds. Many of the photographs in this book are in thanks to him. He has also been instrumental in answering questions and helping to make this book a success.

Some other people that I want to acknowledge come from the Fishers Police Department. George Kehl, the police chief of Fishers for thirty years, provided a lot of information about the history of Fishers and specifically the police department. Jim Suter, the "Major," was deputy chief under Kehl, and we spent a lot of time talking over lunch at the American Legion about history. Former police chief Mitch Thompson, who took over as chief after

Kehl retired, gave me the opportunity to pursue my love of history. I became the department historian and curator and was able to forge partnerships with many other historians and museums across the state. I can't forget to mention Jack Glover, the town's second marshal when it was still a part-time position. Now in retirement, he works at a local liquor store, and I would spend countless hours on a Saturday morning talking with him about the history of the Fishers Police Department.

Those who also contributed to this book are Tom Britt, CEO and founder of Towne Post Network, which publishes the *Fishers Magazine*; C.T.; Rebecca Crowe, librarian at the Fortville-Vernon Township Public Library; Diane Crossley and Mark Rouse with the Fishers Historical Society; John Kautzman with the Ruckelshaus, Kautzman and Blackwell Law Firm; Indiana state senator John Ruckelshaus; Nathan George; and Madalyn S. Kinsey. I want to thank Jim Beehler, a longtime State Farm insurance agent in Fishers. His office was inside Sam Trittipo's building, mentioned later in this book. I want to thank the *Hamilton County Times*, the Michigan State Archives, Indiana State Archives, the Fishers Historical Society, the Carmel-Clay Historical Society, the Indiana State Library, Indianapolis Public Library and the Hamilton County Public Library for their assistance in helping to compile the research needed to write this book. A big thanks to the Log Cabin Animal Hospital for sharing its photos and history of Germantown.

I also want to thank the countless number of Fishers residents who supplied me with many humorous stories that gave me a deeper appreciation for Fishers.

And if it wasn't for Anna Skinner with the *Current in Fishers*, who gave me the opportunity to have my own history column in the paper, this book would probably not have happened.

INTRODUCTION

The history of the city of Fishers can be traced back to 1802 when William Connor settled along the White River and established a trading post. He was the first white settler in this area, and the land that he settled would eventually become the Connor Prairie Living History Park. In 1849, construction began on the Peru & Indianapolis Railroad, which brought more people to the area and led to the creation of New Britton. Then in 1872, Salathial Fisher platted the city along the railroad tracks to capitalize on the economic benefits. The city was originally known as Fishers Switch when a railroad track switch was installed on the line. In 1891, the Indiana General Assembly approved the city as a legal corporation, and it became known as Fishers Station. "Station" was eventually dropped from its name in 1908 by the post office, and the city became known as Fishers.

"Mudsock" was a popular nickname for Fishers. Many people believed that Mudsock was an official name, but many cities throughout the United States have been known as Mudsock. Lack of drainage ditches led to heavily muddied areas in most towns. People would sink down to their ankles, giving them muddy socks, hence the name *Mudsock*. In Fishers, there was even a saloon built on stilts, and on more than one occasion, inebriated patrons would sink all the way down to their knees. It also led to many tall tales like when a man found a hat lying on the road. He picked it up and found a man under the hat. The good Samaritan asked the man, "Can I help you, brother?" The man replied, "No thanks, I am on a horse."

The town of Fishers, looking east, 1924. *Larry A. Reynolds.*

Fishers had a history that is reminiscent of the Wild West. Fishers's rowdy history is mainly attributed to the railroad, which attracted drifters, and its many saloons. Two saloons in Fishers became the site of an infamous fight known as the Battle of Mudsock. But today Fishers is a peaceful town with over ninety thousand residents, which is hard to believe considering that there were only two thousand people in 1980. The boundaries of Fishers were far different than they are today. In order to understand how much Fishers has grown, it is important to know the various cities and towns that have since become extinct but whose remnants live on.

DELAWARE TOWNSHIP

Townships are a local unit of government and a political subdivision of a county. When Fishers was just a small town, it was totally encompassed within Delaware Township. The present size of Fishers now includes Fall Creek Township. When Hamilton County was officially formed in 1822, the county was split into two townships, Delaware in the south and White River township in the north. In 1833, the county split the two townships into nine smaller ones.

The original boundary of Delaware Township extended to Rangeline Road in Carmel, which is in Clay Township. During the 1950s, a school controversy led to the state legislature redrawing the boundary lines. The White River was used as a natural boundary, and Delaware Township went

William Connor's House, located within Connor Prairie Living History Park. *Author's collection.*

from the largest to the smallest in the county. All of Delaware Township west of the White River became part of Clay Township.

Delaware Township may be the smallest of the nine townships, but it has a rich history. Until the courthouse was built in Noblesville, court was held at the house of William Connor. The board of commissioners also met there and made many important decisions affecting the county. Justices of the peace and constables were appointed for the two townships. Noblesville was chosen as the county seat. The first jail, a log building, was built by Josiah Polk on land donated by William Connor on the east bank of the White River. In 1831, the plan for a permanent courthouse was agreed to by the commissioners. Then the county was split into its present nine townships.

FALL CREEK TOWNSHIP

Fall Creek Township was formed in 1833 when Delaware and White River were split. The township was mainly forests, and Indians mostly occupied this area. The first white settler in the township was James McNutt. He was soon followed by other settlers, Hiram Coffee, John Whelchel and Abraham Helms. Living in Fall Creek Township during the early years required courage and endurance to brave the wild that was in stark contrast to Delaware Township.

A funny story was told of Abraham Helms, who was the first man elected justice of the peace in Fall Creek. He was a very religious man. He normally attended events held in the township like log rollings and house raisings. At many of these events, people used profanity, and it was against the law to swear in public. When Fishers was officially incorporated, the town council passed the first eight ordinances on June 21, 1888. The first of these ordinances prohibited swearing in public. Fall Creek Township had a similar law. Since Helms knew it was his duty as justice of the peace to arrest those who swore but understood that these were his neighbors, he made the decision to resign based on conscientious grounds.

Today Fall Creek Township contains Geist Reservoir, many schools and businesses, and it is continuing to grow as Fishers is annexing more land.

NEW BRITTON

In 1851, the Peru & Indianapolis Railroad connected Indianapolis with Noblesville. The railroad line was known as the Nickel Plate. An editor with the *Norwalk Ohio Chronicle* gave the railroad line its nickname because of the amount of money that it would bring in. There were four different lines surveyed and fierce competition not only for the line but also for the cities and towns that would be served by the railroad. The section of the railroad through Fishers has since been replaced with a paved walking trail, but the name Nickel Plate lives on and can be seen everywhere in downtown.

As soon as the railroad was built in 1851, William Brandon founded the town of New Britton. It began to flourish due to its location along the tracks. It wasn't too long before Sam Trittipo arrived and built his mercantile store and became the town's postmaster for nearly twenty years. In 1862, Sydney Cropper bought a farm on the west side of the town and increased the size of the town considerably. Cropper performed the duties of the justice of the peace for a number of years. New Britton was known as "Hell's Half Acre" before the town was able to eliminate most of the whiskey consumption.

The town's "almost" claim to fame came in 1825 when the Indiana legislature was deciding where to relocate the state capitol. The capitol was in Corydon, in southern Indiana, and the lawmakers wanted a more central location. A commission was formed, and William Connor had considerable influence on the members. Connor wanted the state capitol moved to a bluff along the White River not far from his home and less than a mile from New Britton. Connor and the town would stand to benefit financially if they were successful in moving the capitol near the White River. However, the vote was 3–2 in favor of relocating the capitol to Indianapolis, which was considered more geographically center than New Britton. One vote would forever change the destiny of this town.

Once Sam Trittipo moved his store to Fishers Station in 1886, the town of New Britton slowly began to fade away. In 1901, the railroad eliminated the New Britton passenger station, and the town all but disappeared from the map. Today, an elementary school and various neighborhoods continue to honor the legacy of New Britton.

WEST LIBERTY

In Delaware Township, West Liberty was a small Quaker community that was situated between present-day 116th and 96th Streets extending west to the White River. It once had a church, a school, a grocery store and a blacksmith shop. West Liberty even had a horse racetrack—it has since been replaced with the Indianapolis Metropolitan Airport. The track was even rumored to be a possible location for the Indiana State Fair.

Where the name *West Liberty* came from is a mystery. Many American towns were named Liberty, capitalizing on the patriotic fervor of the people. Since there was already a Liberty, Indiana, on the Ohio border, West Liberty may have been a way to distinguish it from the other. The name West Liberty continued to be used until about 1935.

A Quaker church was built in West Liberty near present-day 106th Street and Allisonville Road. It was erected in 1896 with help from the Quaker church in Carmel. The congregation was small like the community, and it lasted until 1918, when membership was transferred to other nearby churches. The church is gone, but a cemetery located nearby lives on, with most of the prominent members of the community interred there.

West Liberty is gone, and there are hardly any signs that it ever existed.

OLIO

The small hamlet of Olio was all that existed in Fall Creek Township. The post office was established on October 22, 1851, and discontinued in 1900. Solomon Cropper, one of the first settlers, petitioned for a post office to be called Lickskillet. The U.S. Post Office Department required that Cropper pick a different name. Lickskillet was a common nickname for over thirty different communities in Indiana. But why he selected Olio is a mystery.

One possible explanation is that the area of Olio was rich in natural resources. Olio was the only town in the state in which every family used natural gas. The name *Olio* is similar to the word *oil*. Many gas companies would come to this area to exploit those natural resources, but Olio would never receive the capital that it should have. Irving Materials Inc. (IMI) operated a quarry on Olio Road, where it mined for limestone, sand and gravel. The retired 230-foot quarry is now being considered as a supplemental water storage for Geist Reservoir.

The U.S. Post Office may have denied the request for the town to be called Lickskillet, but that didn't stop the citizens from using the name. There is a theory of where the name came from. In the olden days, after the family had eaten a meal, the skillet was set outside for the dogs or the deer to lick clean—they were attracted to the salty grease. There is more than one way to clean dishes. Lickskillet came to be known as the "capital" of Fall Creek Township.

Today, Olio lives on as a major road on the eastern side of the city. It crosses over Geist Reservoir and is populated with a number of different schools and businesses.

GERMANTOWN

A small community, Germantown, straddled the Hamilton and Marion County line. It was founded in 1834 as a result of a disagreement over the murder of an Algonquin Indian in the nearby town of Oaklandon in Marion County. Those who disagreed with the murder, mostly German households, moved from Oaklandon and formed Germantown.

In the 1940s, Clarence Geist, president of the Indianapolis Water Company, began to buy up land near Germantown. Plans were made to create a reservoir to supply water to the rapidly growing city of Indianapolis. The residents of Germantown were bought out of their homes, and the land was flooded to create the Geist Reservoir. All that remains of Germantown is lying on the bottom of Geist Lake.

Wicked Fishers tells the stories of murder, bar brawls and grave robbing, along with a few urban legends and ghost stories thrown in. To look at

Aerial view of Fishers, 1977. *Nathan George.*

Fishers today, it is amazing to see how much the city has changed in the last 150 years. For a city as small as it was for more than a century, it made national headlines on more than a few occasions. Fishers may have been small, but it packed a large punch.

1

AN ILLEGAL PRIZE FIGHT

Whoever engages as principal in any prize fight, or attends any such fight as a backer, trainer, second, umpire, assistant or reporter, shall be fined not less than $50 nor more than $500, to which may be added imprisonment in the county jail not exceeding six months.
—Indiana Prize Fighting Statute (1893)

The Club saloon was a downtown Indianapolis bar and gambling house that attracted some of the city's most unsavory characters. Located at 65 North Illinois Street, it was a block away from what would become Indianapolis's most recognized symbol, the Soldier and Sailors Monument. The Hyde Park Prime Steakhouse occupies the site today at the corner of Illinois and Market Streets. It was the type of bar that was frequented by drunkards, gamblers, roughnecks, juvenile delinquents and the common criminal.

On more than one occasion, it was the scene of a murder, and one patron picked the saloon as the ideal place to commit suicide by way of a unique method, ingestion of carbolic acid. It shouldn't have been any surprise when the patrons of the saloon arranged a prize fight in Fishers Station. The bout was hailed as a rematch between two boxers and drew the attention of the local authorities and the ire of the newly elected governor.

In the evening hours of Monday, October 23, 1893, a special train departed Indianapolis headed for Horseshoe Prairie, the first settlement in Hamilton County. Founded less than three years after Indiana became a state, it is now nothing more than an historical memory. Horseshoe Prairie now lies within the boundaries of present-day 160th Street and River Road, stretching west to Allisonville Road near the railroad overpass. About 150 people climbed aboard two coaches, trailed by a baggage car, to witness a prize fight between two boxers, Wiley Evans and Charles Johnson.

Wiley Evans was an African American boxer from California who became a Pacific coast middleweight champion in 1886. He eventually left California and took his fighting to Boston. As Evans had hopes of become a champion boxer, his time in Boston was tumultuous. He acquired the reputation of a quitter and eventually left, establishing his base in Cincinnati.

Charles Johnson was a middleweight boxer from St. Paul, Minnesota, who made his boxing debut in 1888. He made a name for himself winning fights against boxers like Andy Bowen of New Orleans and Jim Burge, the "Cast-Iron man from Australia." Evans was well known in Indiana compared to Johnson. Early in the year, Evans had fought a couple of times at the famous Tomlinson Hall, a 3,500-seat venue, in downtown Indianapolis.

The first fight between Evans and Johnson occurred on Tuesday, September 19, 1893, near Broad Ripple. Word spread fast around Indianapolis that a fight would be taking place, and over 150 people bought tickets for five dollars. However, not everyone showed up to the fight for fear of being arrested for attending an illegal prize fight. Those who were undeterred by criminal prosecution had to go through a series of checks to make sure that undercover police officers didn't sneak into the fight. Attendees had to blink their carriage lights, and a sentry was positioned on the bridge spanning the White River to examine the faces of those attending. Once the prospective attendees were checked, they would be given the exact location of the fight.

The ring was set up on a hill in the middle of a swamp almost totally hidden by the trees surrounding the area. After everyone made their way through the "jungle," the attendees were treated to an exhibition match between Tommy Miller and Charles Vokes before the main event. Although Johnson was relatively unknown, he had the support of the crowd because he was white. Although racial prejudices abounded, the only color that really mattered was green, as hundreds of dollars were wagered on the favorite boxer to win.

The fight lasted nine rounds, with Johnson dominating most of them. In the ninth round, Evans was clearly tired and tried to lock up with Johnson. Evans was thrown off, and Johnson was able to land a punch with his right hand on Evan's jugular. Evans was counted out. Johnson won the purse, taking home $275, and Evans walked away with $25 for his defeat.

After the fight was over, Evans commented that Johnson had fought and won a clean and fair fight. However, that opinion would change. A bitter feud developed between the two boxers in the weeks after. Evans claimed that he lost the fight in Indianapolis because he couldn't get a firm footing in the sand. He asked for a rematch to be held on a floor of "soft poplar." The Club saloon was more than happy to oblige that request.

The train, carrying the boxers and spectators from Indianapolis, arrived in Noblesville, and carriages were waiting to ferry them across the White River to a tent that had been set up for the fight. The location was almost similar to the previous month's fight. A winding path led through a jungle that was lined with ragweed, scrub oak and underbrush while beech and poplar trees hung overhead. It was a perfect night for a fight, with the bright moon giving off just enough light, and the temperature was just cool enough to form dew on the leaves. As the crowd wound its way along the path toward a clearing, a circus tent, highlighted by the moon, loomed high in the distance. The spectators gasped.

After paying the five-dollar admission, the spectators filed into the tent. But the excitement diminished when Hamilton County sheriff Phillip Rhoades and Noblesville city marshal Frank Barnett, along with twenty deputies, arrived to halt the prize fight. The sheriff was tipped off about the upcoming fight, and he refused to allow such an illegal sport to take place within his jurisdiction. The organizers pleaded with the sheriff for over an hour, but it was to no avail. The promoters scrambled to find an alternate location, but they needed a place that would accommodate the crowd. By the time they made it back to the train, word had already spread through Noblesville about the fight. The crowd grew with the addition of Noblesville residents. The promoters were determined to hold this fight, and they knew that they needed a place that would afford little chance of law enforcement interference. That place just happened to be Fishers Station.

Fishers Station was a small town that had a reputation for being rough. The famous Battle of Mudsock had occurred just over a decade before, but the brawl that broke out was still vivid in people's minds. The train arrived in Fishers Station around midnight. Understandably, everyone was irritable and tired, but they were determined to see this fight happen.

The promoters first checked out a camp meeting ground where it was rumored that the platform was big enough to accommodate the fighters and it would adhere to the Queensbury rules. Named after John Douglas, the Ninth Marquess of Queensbury of England, these rules, created in 1867, established the basis of how boxing matches would be fought and are still in use today. Prior to that, boxing was fought under the London Prize Ring rules. Boxing matches were fought bare-knuckled, and there was no limit to the number of rounds that could be fought. It was not uncommon for matches to last forty to fifty rounds, and one match lasted seventy-five rounds. The Queensbury Rules attempted to encourage fair play and sportsmanship.

After walking for nearly a mile, they discovered that the platform was barely large enough to "whip a cat on." Other alternatives were pursued, but Evans refused to fight on anything other than boards, so the crowd sluggishly walked back to the train. They stopped at several barns along the way, but none of the owners would consent. A deserted schoolhouse became the next obvious choice. The first floor was empty, but the upstairs turned out to be a lodge room for the Grand Army of the Republic, a fraternal organization of veterans of the Union army. Just as the room was being rearranged for the fight, a voice yelled out, "Now I will be damned if I'm going to stand here and see this place desecrated by a prize fight." A veteran soldier, who had been standing in the corner, dispersed the crowd, and once again the attendees were forced to head back to the train.

There was no discussion of canceling or postponing the fight, for around 4:00 a.m., they finally found their location. Near the train was a former feed store with a large storeroom big enough to accommodate the fighters and the spectators. Within in an hour, the promoters had set up a ring, layered the floor with resin and installed four gas burners for lights.

Evans entered the ring first, followed by Johnson. After a voice vote was taken, Si Eaglen was chosen as the referee. The boxers were informed of the rules: a twenty-five-round fight, if they tie up with each other, they must break at the signal of the referee and no blows would be struck while they are tied up. Although rules were announced, the fight was touted as a fight with "no fouls." It would have been a bare-knuckled fight, but since the law prohibited it, they used two-ounce gloves instead. The fighters were just as bloodthirsty as the spectators, and they had been waiting for a "good" fight. Good, according to the *Indianapolis News* of October 24, 1893, meant "a fight in which there is absolutely nothing good, but where all the animal antagonism of men is stimulated, and blows are innumerable, and blood is free." The fight between Johnson and Evans was, in this respect, good.

As soon as the bell rang for round 1, Johnson came out of the corner aggressively while Evans seemed to stall for time. Evans got backed into his corner a few times, but the round ended with no damaging effects. Johnson once again came out hard in round 2, landing a punch right on Evan's neck.

Evans returned a punch to Johnson's head and then locked up with him. As soon as they broke, Johnson landed a punch to end the round.

Round 3 saw Evans come out of the corner as the aggressor, with Evans landing a few punches on Johnson's head. Both boxers tied up a half-dozen times and took some cheap shots at each other on the breakaway. Johnson clearly felt the effects of the round. Round 4 saw both fighters equally matched, but they were clearly tired. The round ended with both fighters locked up.

Evans came out swinging in round 5, and his punches were on the mark. Johnson tried to withstand the blows, but Evans landed a hard-right punch, and Johnson fell to the ground. He lay there until the count of nine before he jumped to his feet. Johnson rushed at Evans, knocking him over the ropes. Evans climbed back into the ring, and he drew blood when he landed three punches on Johnson, one to the ribs and two to the face. Evans landed one more punch, and Johnson went down to his knee. Just as Evans had Johnson on the ground, someone in the crowd yelled time. Both fighters went to their corners, but the timekeeper urged them to keep fighting. By the time they realized what had happened, the round was over, and Evans was possibly robbed of a chance at victory.

Surprisingly, Johnson had recovered from the last round, and he landed an uppercut on Evan's neck that set the tone for round 6. When the two boxers came out for round 7, Johnson was once again the aggressor and landed six punches on Evan's breast and neck followed by three uppercuts. They tied up with each other, and on the breakaway, Johnson continued to lay punches until Evans was backed up into his corner. As Evans tried a few evasive maneuvers, Johnson landed a stiff right punch on Evan's jugular. The punch dropped Evans to the ground, and he was counted out. Evans was down on the ground for more than a minute.

Just like the previous fight, Evans admitted defeat, and Johnson walked away with $500 for the victory. After an exhausting night that began in Indianapolis, it was about 5:00 a.m. when the train finally left Fishers Station.

Word of the illegal prize fight spread fast, and the next day it caught the attention of Governor Claude Matthews. He urged the local authorities to prosecute all those who were involved in the fight, including the spectators. Even the railroad wasn't immune, as the Hamilton County prosecutor considered revoking the charter of the Lake Erie and Western Railroad for providing the train cars.

Governor Matthews made it part of his campaign pledge to eliminate prize fighting in the state of Indiana. Upon his swearing in just ten months earlier, the national economy was struck by the Panic of 1893.

Claude Matthews, twenty-third governor of Indiana, 1893–97. *Public domain.*

Unexpectedly, the governor had to deal with rising unemployment, failure of state banks, collapse of land values and labor strikes. But none of that would deter Governor Matthews from making good on his campaign pledge.

Everyone who participated in the prize fight in Fishers Station had every right to be afraid, and they only had to look at what occurred months earlier in Roby, Indiana. The town of Roby, located in Lake County, has since disappeared from the map, but it once was a popular gambling destination. The town had an amphitheater and a racetrack, and directly across the street was an arena that could seat fifteen thousand people. It was reported to be the largest structure of its kind in the United States. Roby slowly acquired the nickname "Monto Carlo of the United States."

Chicago was hosting the World's Fair, and with its close proximity to Roby, the town saw an influx of people who wanted to attend its various venues. Dominic O'Malley of New Orleans formed the Columbian Athletic Club to host prize fights in the new arena. O'Malley, with some assistance, found a loophole in the law that legalized prize fighting.

Soon after Governor Matthews took office, the legislature was in session passing laws. Senator John McHugh of Lafayette introduced a bill giving persons the right to organize associations for the purpose of conducting business, trade or commerce. What the governor failed to read before he signed the bill was that it allowed for organizations to host athletic exhibitions and other physical contests of "science and skill." It is this loophole that allowed O'Malley to circumvent the current law, which levied a fine of at least $50 and no more than $500 and up to six months in jail for anyone engaged in prize fighting.

On June 13, 1893, three thousand spectators were on hand to watch the first athletic contest of "science and skill" in the new arena between Martin Costello and Billy Woods, which ended in a draw after fifty-seven rounds. Governor Matthews was incensed when he heard that the fight had taken place, and he vowed to stop it. Although he regretted signing the McHugh bill, he believed that a court would not see boxing as an athletic contest of skill but for what it really was, a money-making enterprise.

Over the next few months, O'Malley became more brazen and began to advertise his fights in the heart of Indianapolis. He even put up a poster on Market Street, near the entrance to the capitol, knowing the governor would see it on his way to the office. O'Malley began to mock Governor Matthews and even began calling himself "governor." Governor Matthews refused to be made a fool of in his state, especially by someone so conniving as O'Malley.

The next fight at the arena was scheduled for September 4, 1893, between George Lavigne and Young Griffo. Instead of instructing the sheriff of Lake County to enforce the law, as the sheriff failed to do on other occasions, Governor Matthews took matters into his own hand. He felt that a show of force was needed, so he deployed the National Guard to stop the fight. Adjutant General Irvin Robbins deployed four companies of troops: Company F, South Bend; Company K, Frankfort; Company L, Kokomo; and Company G, Rochester. The companies were instructed to meet up at LaPorte, and they would march toward the "enemy." Before the fight was able to begin, seven hundred troops, equipped with twenty-seven thousand pounds of ammunition and two fully loaded Gatlin guns, surrounded the arena. O'Malley, recognizing that the governor was serious, backed down, and the fight was called off. The governor claimed victory.

The next day, a Lake County judge appointed a receiver for the Columbian Athletic Club on the basis that it was violating the law by conducting an illegal business. The arena was now in the possession of the Lake County Sheriff's Department. Governor Matthews did not relent in his pursuit of the Columbian Athletic Club and instead increased the pressure even more.

The next day, after the first fight in the Roby Arena, Costello and Woods, along with the referee, were arrested for prize fighting and released after posting $1,000 bail. They were scheduled to appear in Lake County Circuit Court in the next term, coincidentally the same day that the Indiana militia shut down the arena. Governor Matthews was not satisfied with just charging these three individuals. He called on the governor of New York, Roswell P. Flower, for the extradition of four individuals involved in prize fights at Roby: Solly Smith, John Griffin, Joseph Choynski and Daniel Creedon.

Sensing that the world was crumbling around him, O'Malley attempted to compromise with the governor. He agreed to dispose of his property and leave Indiana if the indictments against him and the other fighters were dismissed. O'Malley would lose about $30,000 on his investment, but the thought of jail was terrifying. But Governor Matthews was not open to compromise, and like the fighters in O'Malley's ring, Matthews had him on the ropes.

Martin Costello was the first person associated with the Roby prize fighting to go on trial on December 11, 1893. He was charged with riotous conspiracy under the act of 1889. However, the defense argued that Costello was innocent based on the Act of 1893, the McHugh bill, making it legal as a showcase of science and skill. The jury disagreed, and after six hours of deliberation, Costello was found guilty. He was sentenced to two years in prison and fined five dollars. His conviction was the first time in the history of the United States that anyone had been sentenced to prison for prize fighting,

The guilty verdict sent shockwaves across the country. It was yet another victory for Governor Matthews in his quest to rid the state of prize fighting. The governor's attention now fell on Fishers Station. It was March 8, 1894, when the Hamilton County grand jury returned indictments against Wiley Evans and Charles Johnson. Although both fighters had been arrested previously in other states for prize fighting, the guilty verdict in the Costello case gave them cause for alarm. Both fighters would have to wait until December to learn that the charges against them were dismissed.

The Roby case still hadn't been settled, and finally on August 21, 1894, a deal was reached where the charges would be dismissed in exchange for pleading guilty to assault and battery. Dominic O'Malley pleaded guilty to two counts and was fined $1,000. Billy Woods and Solly Smith were both fined $300. The referee, Siler, refused to plead, but his case was eventually settled. Charges against all of the others were dismissed. Martin Costello never went to prison. He fled to Canada for a number of years, where he still continued to fight.

Wiley Evans and Charles Johnson continued their boxing careers. Johnson went onto become the World Welterweight Champion in 1895 when he knocked out W. "Cock Robin" Robinson in London before four thousand spectators. But these two fighters would meet one final time. The two boxers were to square off in a ten-round exhibition match in Albany, New York. Johnson once again proved he was the better fighter and laid out Evans after only two rounds.

The Roby case was appealed to the Indiana Supreme Court, and it affirmed that prize fighting was illegal in Indiana. In 1895, Representative Jerome Dinwiddie of Lake County helped repeal McHugh's law, so there would be no confusion on where Indiana stood on prize fighting. After the Costello verdict was handed down, it would take thirty-eight more years before boxing would be legal in Indiana.

2
THE GHOST OF JAMES PAYNE

We have been out here for a while now. I can't but help but feel that somebody has been walking beside us ever since we first started walking. I am hearing leaves rustling on the ground when there is no wind and it kinda seems like it is footsteps and it sounds as if somebody is keeping pace with us with their footsteps.
—Fact or Faked: Paranormal Files *episode "The Caretaker/Cutter," season 1, episode 6*

There is a ghost story in Fishers that tells the tale of a Civil War deserter who haunts a local cemetery. Legend has it that he is the caretaker of the cemetery, keeping watch over the dead as penance for deserting his unit during the war. A good ghost story needs all the right elements, and this one has it all.

Every good ghost story has a unique setting. This story happens to be in a cemetery, but this one is different. Cemeteries in Fishers are maintained by either the Delaware or Fall Creek Township office. They are clearly marked with public access. But this cemetery is different.

Located near the intersection of present day 106th Street and Allisonville Road, is a cemetery practically hidden from the public. It doesn't show up on any maps or even have an official name. Historical records refer to it as the Eller Cemetery for the majority of the Eller family buried there. The nearest landmark is a large fenced-in electrical transformer. From there, a short hike into the woods reveals a cemetery surrounded by galvanized chicken wire.

Grave of James Payne, located in Eller Cemetery in secluded section in Fishers. *Author's collection.*

The star of this ghost story is James Payne. A local Fishers resident, he enlisted in the Union army in August 1861 with Company E of the Thirty-Ninth Indiana Infantry. In September 1862, Payne's unit was engaged in a battle with Confederate forces at Tyree Springs, Tennessee. Military records listed Payne as a deserter, and he was discharged on September 1, 1862. This is where the story begins.

Payne's grave is located in a small corner of the cemetery completely separated from the other headstones. Popular opinion is that placement of his grave was no accident. As a deserter who brought shame upon his family, he was buried in the cemetery away from everyone else. Over time, the story evolved: Payne's ghost hovered over the cemetery as a caretaker, and he was forced to spend eternity keeping watch as punishment for deserting his unit.

The ghost story eventually became the setting of the fictional book *The Ghost of Cheeney Creek* by a local author, Madalyn S. Kinsey. The ghost story garnered national attention when the sci-fi investigative show *Fact or Faked: Paranormal Files* came to Fishers in an attempt to prove if the ghost story was true. A local resident was filming at the cemetery at night when a mysterious person appeared briefly on the tape. The sci-fi investigators used every technique to replicate the image on the video and were unsuccessful. Their conclusion was that the ghost story of James Payne was true.

Now for the rest of the story.

Although James Payne was listed as a deserter, this was corrected later. During the Civil War, many soldiers were listed as deserters when they became separated from their units. It was not uncommon for days, weeks or even months to go by before they found their units again. The desertion charge would be removed as if it never happened. Historical records showed that Payne received a pension until his death, and he attended most of the military reunions with his unit.

The other sign that pointed to Payne not being a deserter was that he was buried with a military headstone. Payne has a Civil War–style headstone that was first designed in 1873 for national cemeteries. Made of marble, the grave marker stands twelve inches high and ten inches wide. The top of the grave is slightly curved with a sunken shield on its face. Inscribed within the shield is the soldier's name and unit, but missing are the soldier's dates of birth and death, which is common on most other graves. Beginning in 1879, the Civil War–style grave was authorized for private cemeteries, and it was only for Union soldiers. Confederate soldiers got a slightly different version. Had Payne actually deserted his unit during the war, he would never have been eligible for a military headstone.

Because of the lack of information and no available dates of birth or death on James Payne, with which to begin a search, the mystery began to swirl. It wasn't long before his desertion led to tales of shame, which led to a great ghost story.

Who was James Payne? There isn't much information. Payne was born in 1823 and was almost forty years old when he enlisted to fight in the Civil War. After his unit was disbanded in 1865, they were welcomed back home to a standing ovation at the statehouse with speeches by the lieutenant governor, General Alvin Hovey, who would later become an Indiana Supreme Court justice and governor.

Payne came back to his native home in Fishers Station. At the age of sixty-four, he became the captain of a constabulary force that had to track down six men, five Black and one white, who got into a fight with a toll gate operator. Payne demonstrated that his age was not a hindrance.

There isn't much information on Payne's early life. He was born in Kentucky in 1823 and was married three times and had one daughter. His second marriage to Eliza Ogle, in 1873, ended in divorce. At the age of eighty-one, he married a widow, Edith Lackey, who was in her sixties. Payne himself would become a widower after only five months when Edith passed away in April 1905. Possibly not wanting to die alone, a few months later, in September, he proposed to marry seventy-eight-year-old Mary Gunion. She had a history of mental illness and had spent time in jail and insane asylums. Payne had already secured the marriage license and scheduled the marriage ceremony. He would return the license to the clerk's office when Mary refused to marry him with no reason for her decision.

After James Payne's rejection at the altar, it would be only a couple more months before he finally met his fate. Payne died on December 12, 1905. His cause of death was listed as nervous frustration with senility, an outdated term that referred to dementia or Alzheimer's disease.

James Payne was buried in the Eller Cemetery with a full military burial. Although commonly referred to as the Eller Cemetery, it was actually a Quaker cemetery. A Quaker church once stood near the corner of present-day 106th Street and Allisonville Road. Originally built in 1890, the advent of the automobile quickly lead to its closure in 1912, and existing church membership was transferred to nearby churches. The cemetery was adjacent to the church, and most of the church members were buried there, including most of the Eller family. Over time, it has come to be known for the Eller family, but actually it is a religious Quaker cemetery. James Payne was also a devout Quaker who decided to be buried near his church.

Although the ghost story of James Payne is entertaining, perhaps the real reason his ghost supposedly haunts the cemetery is that he wants people to know the truth, that he served his country honorably. This doesn't mean that the ghost story isn't true, but that is for the reader to decide.

3
THE LEGEND OF HEADY HOLLOW

Heaven help you if the sun sets on you in Heady Hallow.
—a common quote by residents of the day

Grave robbers. Burned down schoolhouse. Ghosts of weary travelers. Mysterious crashes. What do all of these have in common? They all attempt to explain the origin of Fisher's most haunted location.

Urban legends and ghost stories have been passed down through generations. These stories, whether true or not, help shape a community and give it character. For centuries, there has been one place in Fishers where unusual sounds emanate and ghostly apparitions appear. The area is known as Heady Hollow.

Heady Hollow will not show up on any map, but it isn't hard to find. This haunted area is situated along Allisonville Road, where the road dips at 126th Street before it begins the uphill climb toward 131st Street. While residents still refer to this area as Heady Hollow, pioneer settlers in the early 1800s had a different name: Devil's Land.

The area looks vastly different today than it did in the 1800s. Today, Heady Hollow is a four-lane road lined with houses and subdivisions. But to understand the aura of this haunted area, it requires putting Heady Hollow into perspective. Before Hamilton County was first settled by white settlers in 1818, the Delaware Indians claimed this land as their home.

When William Connor, who settled along the White River, arrived, he immediately made friends with the Indians. He even married one of the members of the tribe. He established a trading post (his land is preserved as part of Connor Prairie History Park), which soon attracted traders in the area. His trading post was just a short distance north of Heady Hollow.

The road that crosses through Heady Hollow became an important link between the city of Noblesville and Indianapolis and for people wanting to do business at Connor's trading post. It was a muddy road, and travelers had to contend with tolls, as most of the roads in Hamilton County were privately owned. But that did not deter them.

Allisonville Road was once lined with elm and catalpa trees, and their leaves and branches formed a canopy over the road. The heart of Heady Hollow is where the road dips at 126th Street as the Big Branch Creek flows underneath toward the White River to the west. Heady Hollow is known for having dense fog, which, combined with windy conditions and encompassing foliage, has given way to some strange encounters and tall tales.

One such story was recounted by a well-known attorney from Noblesville. He was driving his Model T through the Hollow, and standing in the middle of the road was a ghost. He assumed it was one of the many victims that had met their death at the hands of outlaws.

Allisonville Road quickly became an important route for traders. But it also became an ideal road for highwaymen and outlaws to rob and murder unsuspecting travelers. The thick forest surrounding Heady Hollow provided ample cover for robbers looking to prey on innocent victims. It also provided an easy escape route, level terrain at one end or escape by boat on the opposite end. So many people died at the hands of these outlaws that a local attorney, Floyd Christian, commented that the "Hollow often flowed red with blood of God-fearing men who became victims of the bad men of the day." Some people say it is the ghosts of these weary travelers whose restless souls continue to haunt this area of Fishers.

Others claim that the hauntings are ghosts of children who died in a terrible schoolhouse fire. Heady Hollow is named after the Heady family. James Heady settled in Hamilton County in 1825, just a few years after William Connor. He owned an enormous tract of farming land near the Hollow, stretching from 126th Street to 116th Street. Today, the sprawling Sunblest subdivision occupies the area, but the Heady family name lives on. Within the subdivision, there is a street named after them and a small cemetery, conveniently named the Heady Cemetery.

Situated on a hilltop overlooking the Hollow stood a small one-room schoolhouse. It was officially known as Delaware Township School No. 2, but everyone referred to it as the Heady Schoolhouse. The Headys built the school, and most of the students were children of the Heady family. It was more than just a school though. It was also used to hold religious meetings and was an election polling site.

It is unclear exactly when the school was built and when it was demolished, but over the years, stories were passed down describing the fateful day that the schoolhouse caught fire. The fire was intense, and it spread quickly. The children were inside at the time and unable to get out before the fire consumed them. The community was devastated that so many young children perished; it was one of the most awful tragedies that had ever occurred in this small town.

This would have been a tragic story, if only it were true. There is no record of the school ever burning down. The most tragic thing that ever befell the school was vandals breaking in and destroying desks and books. It is anyone's guess how this story came to be, but it is one that has been passed down for generations. Now the ghosts of dead children occupy the haunted area of Heady Hollow.

Heady Schoolhouse, No. 2. *From the* Noblesville Ledger, *June 4, 1979.*

But the Legend of Heady Hollow doesn't stop with victims who met their demise on the highway or with children burned in a fire. Another explanation is that the area is haunted by restless souls who were raised prematurely out of the ground. Residents claim that grave robbers and "resurrectionists" are to blame for the hauntings at Heady Hollow. But unlike the previous explanations, this one has a semblance of truth.

At the turn of the twentieth century, medical schools in Indianapolis were paying people to dig up bodies to be used as cadavers. These individuals were known as "ghouls." There was an infamous resident in Fishers, Hampton West, who engaged in grave robbing. He was eventually charged and sentenced to ten years in the Indiana State Prison. His trial made big headlines, and it forced the state legislature to take action to prevent this from happening again and to establish a legal way for medical schools to get cadavers.

But the story of the hauntings of Heady Hollow does not center on Hampton West but rather on Ebenezer Heady, who is a ghost himself. He is perhaps based on the true-life persona of West, but there is no record that an Ebenezer Heady ever existed. Legend has it that Ebenezer was a grave robber who never shied away from making an easy dollar. He dug up one too many graves, and his last dig, unbeknownst to him, was the grave of his young son. Seeing his dead son in the coffin drove him mad, and he lived out the rest of his days insane. (Hampton West dug up the grave of his niece, but it didn't faze him in the slightest.) The ghosts of Ebenezer and the victims that he disturbed from their final resting place are those believed to wander the area of Heady Hollow.

The ghost stories may have been an attempt to explain the unusual occurrences and the high number of accidents in the Hollow. There were reports of horses being spooked for no reason, causing damage to the carriages and severely injuring the occupants. Vehicle accidents, especially head-on collisions, were common, and many vehicles found their way into the creek bed below.

Whether the accidents were due to driver error or some supernatural force, the county commissioners decided that Heady Hollow was one of the most dangerous places on the road stretching from Noblesville to Indianapolis. So in 1923, the area of Heady Hollow was lined with three foot posts to prevent vehicles from running off the road. It didn't help.

So the aura surrounding Heady Hollow continues to fascinate, and its significance is more predominant during Halloween. Whether the haunted stories are true or not, it is a part of the fabric of this community, and the legend of Heady Hollow lives on.

4
FALL CREEK INDIAN MASSACRE

Let them be sworn—nobody but a lawyer would defend a murderer.
—Judge Winchell referring to swearing in the attorneys who would be representing the accused

Before Indiana became a state, Fall Creek Township was nothing more than unbridled wilderness. It took an enormous amount of courage to brave the harsh environment. Wild animals ruled the area with total abandon. To survive in this section of the county required courage and determination and a willingness to overcome obstacles.

Thorpe Creek is a small stream flowing through the township. The Thorp brothers settled along the stream briefly before moving farther westward. Their brief visit would end up as an enduring legacy, as the stream was eventually named for them.

James McNutt, an Irishman, was the first permanent white settler in Fall Creek Township. He was also the first person from the township to be sued civilly in the Circuit Court of Hamilton County for trespass. Shortly after arriving in the township, McNutt came upon two cabins that appeared to have been abandoned. It was unclear how long they had been there, but they were built close to Thorpe Creek. The mystery about who built the cabins persisted. Was it the Thorp brothers or was it the Indians, although it wasn't something that they would have built? Unbeknownst to McNutt and the other few settlers, the cabins contained a dark secret.

The cabins were built by Andrew Sawyer and John Bridge in 1821. They were in-laws, as Sawyer's sister was married to Bridge. One cabin was built on the south bank of Fall Creek near the mouth of Thorpe's Creek while the other cabin was built on the north bank. They were frequent traders with William Connor, the first white settler in what would become Delaware Township. Connor and his brother, John, arrived in Hamilton County in 1800, more than a decade before the area would officially be known as Hamilton County. Most of Indiana was still under the control of Native Americans, and the few white settlers had to find a way to live in harmony.

In 1818, with the signing of the Treaty of St. Mary's in Ohio, six different Indian tribes ceded their land to the United States. At the negotiations, William Connor acted as an interpreter. He had been married to an Indian woman, Mekinges, for sixteen years. She was the daughter of Chief Kikthawenund, more commonly known as William Anderson. (The city of Anderson is named for him.) Chief Anderson, representing the Delaware tribe, urged the Indians to agree to the terms of the treaty. This meant that the Indians, including Connor's wife and six children, would be forced to move west. Connor decided against going with his wife and children and instead stayed where he was, as he had a very profitable trading post.

By 1821, when Sawyer and Bridge built their cabins, most of the Indian population had already moved westward, but there were still some who refused to leave. For the most part, there were not many clashes between the white settlers and the Indians. Quite the opposite, there was a lot of mutual cooperation, and both groups profited through trade, although each viewed the other with a watchful eye. But on March 22, 1824, a major incident between white settlers and Indians would become a national issue and something that had never happened in the United States up to that point.

Hamilton County had just become official in 1822, and the year after, Madison County was officially formed. Pendleton was the county seat, with only a few houses located near the falls. (Anderson was just a small village, but the county seat would eventually be moved there.) These counties were still in their infancy.

A group of Seneca Indians—two men, three women and four children—was encamped on the east side of Fall Creek, about eight miles upstream from where Bridge and Sawyer lived. The small tribe was led by two Indians, Ludlow and Mingo. They knew most of the white settlers they traded with, so that helped to east tensions. But there were some white settlers who always made the Indians feel uneasy.

One particular night, the Indians were gathered around the campfire enjoying one another's company when through the woods appeared five white men: Thomas Harper, James Hudson, Andrew Sawyer, John Bridge and his eighteen-year-old son, John Bridge Jr. The Indians had a reason to be suspicious of this group. Hudson had accused Ludlow of threatening to kill white men for disturbing his traps. But there was also a rumor that Ludlow, in a drunken rage, drew a knife and threatened to kill Hudson's wife.

When the party of white men showed up at the encampment, Thomas Harper put all suspicion to rest when he shook Ludlow's hand. Harper explained that two of his horses ran off and they could use Ludlow and Mingo's help in finding them. They would each be paid a fee of fifty cents. The Indians sensed no danger, and as fifty cents was a lot of money, they agreed.

After about a mile trek through the woods, they took a break to rest. The white men offered to share their whiskey with the Indians. Mingo declined, but Ludlow had several rounds. After the brief interlude, and the nice gesture of sharing their whiskey with the Indians, it was time to resume the search for the missing horses. They separated into two groups. Mingo went with Hudson, Jones and Bridge Jr. Ludlow would go with Harper, Sawyer and Bridge Sr.

As Mingo was walking through the woods, he failed to notice that his white companions had fallen back. Then a gunshot rang out somewhere in the woods. Realizing that was the sign, the three white men raised their guns at Mingo and fired. Jones and Bridge Jr.'s guns misfired, but fortunately for them, Hudson's did not. Before Mingo could turn around, the bullet struck him in the back, exiting his chest and leaving a gaping hole in his body. Still clinging to life, Mingo screamed, "You kill me." Bridge Jr. jammed the butt of his rifle into Mingo's chest. Jones tried to finish Mingo off with the muzzle of his weapon only a few inches from his face. Mingo begged, "If you shoot me, shoot me through my head." Jones's weapon once again misfired, so Bridge Jr. clubbed Mingo to death with his rifle.

The gunshot that was originally heard through the woods was Ludlow meeting the same fate as Mingo. The white men fell back, and with Ludlow's back turned, they fired, killing him instantly.

With Ludlow and Mingo dead, the group of white settlers reassembled. The decision was made that all of the Indians, including the children, needed to be killed. Upon returning to the camp, the women were naturally concerned by the gunshots and the fact that Ludlow and Mingo were not with them. After they were assured that they would be returning soon, one of the women turned her back to the white men. Bridge Sr. raised his rifle and shot her in the back. While she was pleading for her life, one of the men crushed her skull. Sawyer shot and killed another woman. Then eighteen-year-old Bridge Jr. killed the last one.

All that remained were the children, two ten-year-old boys and two girls probably around five. As the little ones were defenseless, the white men slaughtered the children using rifles, tomahawks and knives. The two girls and one boy lay dead, but one of the boys was still alive. Sawyer grabbed the boy by the ankles and swung him. His head hit the end of a fallen log, and his brains lay scattered among the wood.

The men then stole everything from the camp and proceeded back to their cabin in Fall Creek Township. The perpetrators probably believed that their crime would never be solved or that if it was known, the white population would be sympathetic to them. The U.S. government taking away the Indians' land and the domination of the white race over the Natives seemed logical; they would not be held accountable for their crimes. Thomas Harper, probably sensing exactly the opposite, fled to Ohio and would never be held accountable for his role in the massacre.

However, that was far from the case. Madison and Hamilton Counties still had sizeable Indian populations, and once the details of the massacre started to spread, tensions rose. The Indians wanted justice, and the white residents were concerned of Indian retaliation. Details of the massacre were relayed to Colonel John Johnston at the Indian Agency in Piqua, Ohio. The agency then sent the information to the War Department in Washington, D.C.

When Colonel Johnston arrived in Madison County, he requested that William Connor assist him. Because of his experience with the various Indian tribes, he was needed to mediate the situation and prevent any more bloodshed. They would visit every Indian tribe in the area to reassure them that the offenders would be punished and asked for their promise that they would not take matters into their own hands. The Native Americans agreed, and the white settlers were able to breathe a sigh of relief.

Once the murderers were identified, Madison County sheriff Samuel Cory arrested them and confined them in a square log jail. The prisoners wore iron restraints attached to a floor covered with straw. The trial would be held in Pendleton in a newly built log cabin. One room would be utilized for the court, while the other room was for the grand jury.

The court was composed of three judges. The presiding judge, William Wick, had been elected as the Hamilton County circuit judge in 1823. At the time, Madison County fell under the jurisdiction of the Hamilton County courts. Judge Wick was young, but he was also knowledgeable in criminal law. Wick was assisted by two associate judges, Samuel Holliday and Adam Winchell. Holliday was well respected, but Winchell was devoid of any legal experience. He was a blacksmith who had forged the irons that the suspects were currently wearing. He was described as honest, rough and illiterate—not quite what one would expect of a judge.

Moses Cox was Madison County's first clerk, who many said could barely write his own name. Sheriff Cory would ensure law and order was maintained during the trials. Colonel Johnston would ensure that witnesses were paid for their time. The prosecuting attorney for Madison County was Calvin Fletcher, a competent attorney but young. Sensing that this was going to be a high-profile trial, the War Department instructed U.S. senator General James Noble to prosecute the case. Noble picked his son-in-law, Phillips Sweetzer, to assist him.

The first of the men to go on trial was James Hudson. The first day drew many distinguished attorneys from as far as Ohio, as this case was indeed shaping up to be one for the ages. One person was clearly absent at the start of the trial, the presiding judge, William Wick. Hudson's attorney, William Morris, saw an opportunity to take advantage of the Judge Winchell's lack of legal knowledge.

"I move the court for a writ of habeas corpus." Morris was referring to the writ that allows a person to challenge the reasons or conditions of a person's confinement.

Judge Winchell, clearly having no idea what Morris was talking about, responded, "What do you want to do with it?"

"To bring up the prisoners and have them discharged," replied Morris.

Showing his ignorance, Winchell asked, "Is there any law for that?"

Morris must have been beside himself, but he acquiesced and read the statute describing a writ of habeas corpus.

Judge Winchell informed Morris, "That act has been repealed long ago."

Shocked, Morris replied, "Your honor is mistaken, it is a constitutional writ, as old as the Magna Carta itself," referring to the royal charter of England created in 1215, which was written into the U.S. Constitution.

To put the matter to rest, Judge Winchell responded, "Well, Mr. Morris, to cut the matter short, it would do you no good to bring out the prisoners. I ironed them myself and you will never get them irons off until they have been tried, habeas corpus or no habeas corpus. Motion denied."

Judge Wick entered the courtroom just as the legal circus ended.

James Hudson was brought into the court, and his appearance was vastly different from when he was first arrested. He was pale, disheveled and his voice cracked as he pleaded not guilty. The jury looked far different than it does today. The all-male jury comprised rugged pioneers all wearing moccasins and armed with knives attached to their sides. The charge of murder was announced, and the evidence against Hudson was presented to the jury.

Hudson tried to appeal to the jury's prejudice against the Indians. He told of stories of massacres of white people by the Indians and recounted tales from Daniel Boone. He was no match against General Noble, who hammered home the virtues of justice, patriotism and love of the law while holding up the bloody clothes worn by the Indians at the time of their murder. Even the crowd was moved by Noble's forcible speech.

Once both sides were done presenting, Judge Wick instructed the jury in his own eloquent way. He impressed upon the jury members that "the law knew no distinction as to nation or color; that the murder of an Indian was equally as criminal in law as the murder of the white man." The next morning, the jury returned a verdict of guilty of murder in the first degree. Hudson, with his head hanging down, heard the judge pronounce a sentence of death to be carried out in a few days.

The gallows were erected near the north side of the falls. The execution drew an even larger crowd than the trial. Among the crowd were several Seneca Indians, mostly relatives of the deceased. Hudson made one last atonement for his sins and pleaded for mercy and his life to be spared. Mercy was denied, and as the floor gave way, the rope snapped his neck. Hudson's lifeless body twisted while suspended in the air.

This was the first time anywhere in the United States that a white man was hanged for the killing of an Indian. It would be about five months later that Andrew Sawyer, John Bridge and his son would have their day in court. At the conclusion of Hudson's execution, it was decided to postpone the other trials until the start of the next court term. It must have been painful to sit around and wait, wondering if the same fate that befell Hudson would also be applied to them.

Spring finally arrived and with it many changes from when Hudson was tried the previous year. The Indiana legislature attached Madison County to the third judicial circuit, which would provide a new judge and prosecutor. Judge Miles Eggleston replaced Judge William Wick, and Oliver H. Smith, prosecutor for the third judicial circuit and future U.S. senator, replaced General Noble as the lead prosecutor. Noble and his son-in-law would stay on to assist. The associate judges, sheriff, court clerk and attorneys for the accused remained unchanged.

Andrew Sawyer was tried first for the killing of one of the women at the camp. The trial process was almost identical to Hudson's trial. The evidence was overwhelming. Sweetzer, Noble's son-in-law, gave the opening speech for the state. Three powerful speeches from the defense, William Morris, Charles H. Test and James Rariden, advocated for Sawyer. General Noble closed the case for the state.

After a half day of deliberation, the court returned a verdict of guilty of manslaughter, and Sawyer was sentenced to two years of hard labor in the penitentiary. But the proceedings weren't over. He immediately went on trial again, this time for the murder of one of the young boys.

Oliver Smith would handle this part of the case. In his memoirs, he wanted to make the distinction between the two cases for the jury; there is a difference between manslaughter and murder. The heinous act of smashing the boy's head against a log was cold-blooded murder. Smith took an hour to hammer his point home to the jury. The boy's blood-soaked shirt lay across the table for the jurors as he spoke.

Then, in a dramatic fashion, Smith held up the bloody shirt and told the jury:

> *Yes, gentlemen of the jury, the cases are very different. You might find the prisoner guilty of only manslaughter, in using his rifle on a grown squaw* [woman]*; that was the act of a man, but this was the act of a demon. Look at that shirt, gentlemen, with the bloody stains upon it; this was a poor helpless boy, who was taken by the heels by this fiend in human shape, and his brains knocked out against a log! If the other case was manslaughter, is not this murder?*

The members of the jury, heavily bearded men of rugged natures, who never showed emotion, were all weeping. It took only a few minutes to return a verdict of guilty of murder in the first degree. Sawyer was sentenced to death.

The trial of John Bridge Sr. would commence the following morning. He was on trial for the murder of one of the young girls. His trial was no different than Sawyer's second, and a verdict of guilty of murder in the first degree was returned within a few minutes.

The last person to be tried was eighteen-year-old John Bridge Jr. for the murder of the second boy at the camp. Like the two before him, a verdict of guilty of murder in the first degree was returned. His sentence was the same, death by hanging. However, the court recommended to the governor of Indiana a pardon because of his age.

Like Hudson before them, the gallows were erected in the same spot to carry out the executions of Sawyer, the elder Bridge and his son. The governor had not sent word that he was granting a pardon, so the executions of all three proceeded.

Thousands had gathered to watch the executions. A Seneca chief, along with most of his tribe, was in attendance. Sawyer and the senior Bridge would be the first two to be executed. John Bridge Jr. watched from the side as his uncle and father were hanged for all of the crowd to see. The audience was in tears, and the Senecas expressed their satisfaction that justice had been served.

After an hour, the bodies were brought down and laid in coffins. It was now time for the younger Bridge to ascend the scaffolding to meet the same fate. He was so weak and scared that the sheriff had to assist him onto the platform and adjust the rope around his neck. With the rope attached, he looked down and saw his uncle and father lying peacefully in their coffins and knew that this terrible ordeal would soon be over.

But at the last minute, Governor James B. Ray, who was in attendance at the execution, granted his pardon to John Bridge Jr. Ray had just become governor a couple of months earlier, and he was the youngest governor in Indiana history, taking office one week before his thirty-first birthday. Perhaps sensing that he was not that much older than Bridge Jr. and he had a long life ahead of him, the governor showed compassion for the young man. The crowd exhaled at the announcement and heartily agreed with the governor; however, they were dismayed that he waited until the rope was already around the boy's neck.

This ended the last of the trials of the white men for the killing of the Indians. With the assistance of William Connor and the swift justice that was meted out to the murderers, it prevented more bloodshed and retaliation and now life could resume as it was before the murders.

After his pardon, John Bridge Jr. left Indiana and went back to Butler County, Ohio, to work with his family on their farm. In 1834, he got married and came back to Indiana, this time settling in Carroll County. He would live nearly half a century in Indiana as a prosperous merchant. In 1872, near the age of sixty-seven, he returned to the falls for the first time since his father met his death. Four years later, Bridge died and was buried in Delphi, Indiana.

When the first white settlers in Fall Creek Township came upon these two cabins built along Thorpe Creek, they would never have guessed that it was the starting point of one of the worst massacres in Indiana history and that it would lead to the first execution of a white man for the killing of an Indian.

5

JUNCTION 69

I'm a Baptist, I'm a Mason, and a Shriner. All I'm trying to do is satisfy red-blooded farmers and workers who like the female anatomy and a few drinks. We don't do anything illegal.
—Clare Stimson, owner of Junction 69

Fishers has always been a town that prides itself on its midwestern values. It's a town where everyone knows one another and they're always willing to help out their neighbors. It's a town that emphasizes the importance of family and encourages citizens to uphold the town's values.

So in 1981, when an adults-only strip club establishment, Junction 69, opened up in the center of town, the citizens were in shock. The owner of the bar, Clarence "Clare" Stimson, would eventually find himself in a legal battle with the Fishers Town Council. And if that wasn't enough, he would also have to wage a morality war with a local religious group. This is the story of one man's battle to keep his business against a town that refused to let its values be compromised.

Up until the opening of Junction 69, the biggest nuisance that Fishers had to contend with was the drunks and fights that occurred at the Fishers Tavern, the local bar in town. The tavern was also the scene of a few shootings. The Fishers Tavern (located at the present-day site of the Nickel Plate Bar) had a long history dating back to the early 1900s. And although its reputation became a negative one, it wasn't always bad.

The Fishers Tavern was a popular spot for the locals to have a drink and socialize. On any given day, the hitching post outside would be overcrowded with horses ready to carry their inebriated owners home. In 1920, Albert Trittipo turned half of the Fishers Tavern into an ice cream parlor, making it a popular spot for the children.

In the 1930s, the Fishers Tavern became the social center of town. Families would gather to listen to live bands or movies shown on the outside walls. The new owner behind all this, Ira Spealman, had grand ideas to draw people to the tavern. He once hired a performer to walk a tightrope that stretched from the bank to the grain elevator. As everyone gathered to watch the circus act, the performer got stage fright and backed out.

This was more or less how the Fishers Tavern operated for many years. Beginning in the 1970s, the tavern's reputation turned for the worse. The tavern was routinely cited and investigated by the Indiana Excise Police for illegal sale of alcohol to minors. Fights would routinely break out, and it no longer resembled the friendly tavern of its former years.

Things finally came to a head in the early morning hours of Friday, May 16, 1975. At 3:30 a.m., the tavern owner, Robert Woolum, had just closed up and was carrying $500 from that night's deposit. He was approached by three men in the parking lot. A few days before, a nearby business had been burglarized, and the liquor store next to the tavern had been robbed a few months earlier. Fearing he was going to be robbed, he drew a .44-caliber magnum revolver and fired a warning shot. As the subjects continued to advance, Woolum fired once again, striking Carl Hall Jr. in the stomach.

Fishers's town marshal, Jack Glover, investigated the incident. It was determined that Woolum fired without reason and was charged with assault with a deadly weapon with the intent to kill. A year later, a jury deliberated for seven hours, declaring Woolum guilty for aggravated assault. Hamilton County judge V. Sue Shields sentenced Woolum to one to five years in prison. The tavern was put up for auction.

Questions began to swirl when Clare Stimson bought the Fishers Tavern at auction in the winter of 1975. As the ninth owner of the tavern, many doubted that Stimson could turn it around and others had hoped that the tavern would never reopen.

Clare Stimson was a true entrepreneur. A Gary native, he moved to Indianapolis from South Bend in 1973. While working for Allstate, he had worked his way up the corporate ladder, and many people believed that he could have been president of the company. But Clare Stimson had grown tired of the 8–5 work schedule and corporate America. At the core of his being, he was a people person and he wanted a job that would satisfy that need.

A graduate of Indiana University with a degree in psychology, Stimson walked away from a corporate job to invest in a liquor store. He quickly realized that owning a liquor store did not satisfy his need to interact with people. So when the Fishers Tavern was put up for auction, he knew that being a tavern owner was his calling.

Clare Stimson knew that challenges lay ahead if he reopened up the Fishers Tavern. So he decided to make some drastic changes. He moved the Fishers Tavern from the location it occupied for nearly a century to a couple of blocks east at 8772 116th Street (present-day location of Handel's Ice Cream). The one-hundred-year-old house with an attached metal building was formerly a carpet sales office and warehouse. The new bar would be housed in the metal warehouse building with plans to renovate the house into a restaurant. But moving the bar was not enough. The Fishers Tavern name had become toxic, so in addition to a new location, the bar finally had a new name, Clare's Pub.

Clare's Pub officially opened on July 1, 1976. A wooden Indian stood outside to greet customers. Inside, the bar looked nothing like its predecessor. The walls were covered with tulip poplar, Indiana's state tree. The square bar sat on a raised platform, while the center pit was sunken down. Stimson designed it this way so the bartender and the customer were always at eye level. Music performers played on a stage that was tucked in the corner surrounded by an old cemetery fence. The front doors of the pub once belonged to an Indianapolis morgue. Food service was limited, but according to Stimson, Clare's Pub had the "best ham sandwich in the state."

It appeared that Stimson was successful in shedding the bad image of the Fishers Tavern. Clare's Pub had become a place where locals could relax and unwind after a long day. It was a place where farmers, men in suits and long-haired youth all became friends if only for a short time. Clare Stimson described it like so: "This is a place where their real humanity comes out. It's a melting pot of farmers, lawyers, and laborers, bankers, builders, dreamers, and fools. There are poor and super-rich, the genuine fun loving and super-patriots."

It wasn't long before the honeymoon phase came to an end. By 1979, the bar's reputation began to take on its predecessor's. The bar was subjected to fourteen raids in just three months. The raids and negative publicity began to affect Stimson's profits. The bar had been purchased

Clare Stimson shares his pub in Fishers with unpretentious patrons and this antique wooden friend. — The NEWS Photo, Joe Young.

Clare Stimson standing outside Fishers's only strip club, Junction 69. *From the* Indianapolis News, *October 12, 1978.*

with a $65,000 loan from the Small Business Administration in December 1975. After falling behind on the loan payments, Stimson made a decision to recoup his losses. But that decision would turn the town against him and set up a battle for morality.

In November 1980, Clare's Pub closed down for a month for renovations. When it reopened, the bar was now a strip club, a go-go bar, in the heart of downtown Fishers. In fact, it was the only strip club in Hamilton County. The bar underwent another name change, Junction 69. The club's name became popular for various reasons, but it was actually named for Interstate 69 located nearby.

Inside the new establishment, four dancers would take turns dancing on a red-carpeted elevated stage. Live music had been replaced with a jukebox; dancers picked their songs before going on stage. Indiana's strict public indecency laws prevented the performers from getting totally nude, and even their nipples had to be covered. Most of the patrons were young men and occasionally a few couples.

As soon as the red light on the building advertising "Junction 69 Go-Go Girls" lit up, a plan was in motion to shut down the bar. While the bar was under renovations in November, rumors were circulating around town that it would reopen as a strip club. The Fishers Town Council met that same month and passed a new rezoning ordinance. The ordinance rezoned the area surrounding the club, which would prohibit the sale of alcoholic beverages.

Clare Stimson argued that the new zoning ordinance should not apply because ownership of the bar never changed; therefore, he was exempt because of the grandfather clause. Other bars in the area were protected, but the town disagreed with Stimson. Because the bar's use changed from a tavern to a cabaret, the bar was not grandfathered and he must file an appeal with the Fishers Plan Commission within fifteen days or close its doors.

The town maintained that the timing of the new ordinance was purely coincidental and it had nothing to do with Junction 69. However, Stimson believed that the town had a vendetta against him. From the unfounded raids to the police harassment on New Year's Eve 1979, when the police scared off customers by parking across the street, Clare Stimson had had enough of the town's politics.

A showdown was scheduled at Fishers Town Hall on February 11. Stimson refused to attend the hearing, and the board of zoning appeals forwarded the violations to the Fishers Town Council. The attendance at the hearing was surprisingly sparse, as the real showdown was being held right outside of Junction 69.

Religious groups and churches in town were already putting extreme pressure on local politicians to take action against Junction 69. Noblesville and Carmel were already examining their own ordinances to make sure strip clubs didn't show up in town like Junction 69 did in Fishers. When Ronald Reagan was elected president, he was helped into office by a new religious movement. Reverend Jerry Falwell noticed that America was in a moral decline. Abortion, pornography and homosexuality were social topics that conservative groups believed were harming America. In response, Falwell created the Moral Majority, a political organization affiliated with the Christian Right and the Republican Party. Eventually, states began to form their own chapters, with Indiana being one of the first.

A local church affiliated with the Moral Majority, the Noblesville Baptist Temple, set its sights on Junction 69 and staged a protest during the same

Protest on a cold evening in front of Junction 69, a topless bar. *From the* Noblesville Ledger, *December 31, 1981.*

time as the zoning hearing. About fifty-two members of the church, including toddlers and young children, carried placards with Bible verses as they marched in the blistering cold. Five police cars met the church bus as they arrived in front of the bar. The protest lasted only fifteen minutes as the negative-36-degree winds brought it to a premature close.

The church pastor, Ken Roberts, said the bar was a promoter of sin and polluted the minds of young people. He said the protest was to "make decency known." The bar was ready for the protesters, and the new manager of the bar, John Victory, had a message of his own. On a lighted sign, it read "Junction 69—God Bless America, Land of Freedom." A petition was signed by over seventy residents that supported the town's new zoning laws. Fishers town marshal George Kehl said that the town was not ready for a strip club.

At the next Monday's council meeting, Clare Stimson was given an ultimatum to meet with the town attorney within seven days to work out an agreement or risk having the bar closed down. The town board president, Stephen Brooks, didn't see much of a chance for a compromise and knew

A "for sale" sign is displayed outside the Junction 69 strip club. *From the* Noblesville Ledger, *May 8, 1981.*

that the only other course was to deal with it in court. Stimson refused to comply, and the Town of Fishers filed a lawsuit on March 3 to declare that Junction 69 was operating illegally.

The case would never make its way to court. Clare Stimson started to receive death threats if he didn't close the bar down. On March 20, the bar's manager, John Victory, was shot in the hand as he stood in the parking lot after closing up the bar. Peaceful protests had turned criminal.

Five days later, on March 25, two Sheridan men were inside the bar. One of them spit on a dancer, and they fought the bouncers as they were being escorted out of the building. They went out to their car and fired three rounds into the building. One of the bullets missed a dancer's head by inches and was found lodged in the wall. The suspects fled in a blue 1966 Chevrolet. They were apprehended by Fishers deputy marshal Jim Suter and Hamilton County sheriff's deputy Thurl Cecil. Both subjects were charged with criminal recklessness and attempted battery using a deadly weapon.

In the wake of the shooting, Clare Stimson closed the bar down for a cooling-off period. He was preparing for a "grand opening" on Friday, April 10, but that would not happen. On April 8, the bar closed indefinitely. After months of harassment, threats and civil litigation, Clare Stimson had enough of the Fishers "vigilantes." There were rumors of an attempt on his life. An anonymous caller called Fishers Town Hall threatening to burn down Junction 69.

Stimson told a reporter on the phone, "I'm so sick and tired of the threats and violence that I do not care to do business in Fishers. I'm gone. You won't see me in Fishers. I won't get shot in Fishers." He planned to sell the bar and his home but vowed to continue the legal fight against the town. Although Fisher's only strip club lasted just a few months, it showed what the power of community can accomplish when people come together for a common cause.

6

THE BATTLE OF MUDSOCK

I am the best damned man in Mudsock and can whip any son of a bitch in it.
—Benjamin Fouch, November 19, 1881

Most of the residents of Fishers Station had gathered together on a cold brisk Sunday morning in December to hear a sermon by the well-known Methodist preacher Thomas Goodwin. Based in Indianapolis, Goodwin traveled the state preaching his famous sermons on temperance and the evils of drunkenness. Goodwin had felt compelled to visit the small town of Fishers Station because of the awful tragedy that occurred there about two weeks before.

In 1881, Fishers Station was just shy of a decade old and numbered just under two hundred people. But the town was growing due to its stop on the Indianapolis, Peru and Chicago Railroad line. The railroad helped increase commerce. The small town boasted two sawmills, one flouring mill, two dry good stores, one drugstore, two blacksmith shops, one wagon shop and one tile factory. The town seemed poised for greatness, if it wasn't for two saloons straddling the railroad tracks.

This small town would soon make headlines across the nation. The headlines read, "A Fight Among Ruffians," "Fighting Whiskey," "A Saloon-Keepers War," "Hostile Hoosiers" and "Massacre in Indiana." In less than three weeks, the news would make its way across the Atlantic to England. The incident seemed to suggest the reputation of states like Missouri and Texas would "tremble for fear the laurels will be snatched

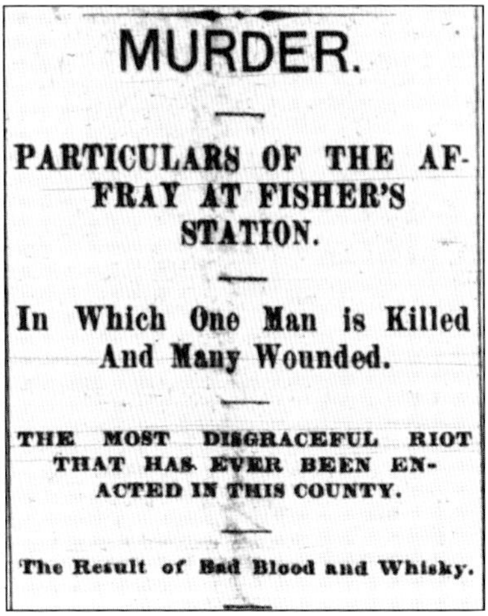

MURDER.

PARTICULARS OF THE AFFRAY AT FISHER'S STATION.

In Which One Man is Killed And Many Wounded.

THE MOST DISGRACEFUL RIOT THAT HAS EVER BEEN ENACTED IN THIS COUNTY.

The Result of Bad Blood and Whisky.

Front page headline about the Battle of Mudsock. *From the* Ledger, *November 25, 1881.*

from their brows." Hard to believe that this nationally recognized incident started over something so trivial.

Saturday, November 19, 1881, started off like any other day. The saloons were packed with patrons getting their fill of whiskey. It wasn't quite noon yet, and most everyone was already drunk. The saloons were basically twenty-four-hour establishments. They operated from 5:00 a.m. until 11:00 p.m. but that doesn't mean that they quit serving. Patrons sometimes would continue to drink into the morning hours. The desire to make more money sometimes outweighed the penalty, which ranged anywhere from ten to fifty dollars. The Farrell brothers, Andy and Ed, would flirt with the law occasionally. They were currently appealing their fine of twenty-eight dollars handed down by Squire Caylor the previous month. The Farrell saloon would become the starting point for the most "disgraceful" affair to have ever occurred in Hamilton County.

Sometime before noon in Farrell's saloon, a disagreement between two men set in motion a series of events that would forever put Fishers Station on the map. The railroad occasionally brought unsavory characters to Fishers Station. A drifter nicknamed "Dutch Joe" got into an argument with a local farmer, Barney Reiner. What led to the argument is unknown, but it is presumed that one of them spoke ill of the quality of the whiskey.

The argument between the two men would continue up until noon, when it seemed that the disagreement had been put to rest. Shortly after noon, the argument resumed, and then it turned physical. Reiner was declared the victor, and Dutch Joe was sent packing with his tail between his legs. The patrons in the bar began to take sides, those backing Reiner and those backing Dutch Joe.

The whiskey continued to flow like water, and between four and five o'clock, the feud from that afternoon's fight came to a head. The Lynn brothers—Daniel, Wesley and Adam—were playing a game of pool with their good friend, Benjamin Fouch. The Lynn brothers were from Castleton, a few miles south of Fishers Station.

Fouch was from Indianapolis and had once been a Marion County deputy sheriff, under Sheriff John Tressley. Fouch was known to have a bad temper and was prone to fighting, especially when under the influence of whiskey. His temper is what probably ended his law enforcement career. He would end up working odd jobs to make a living. He once lived in Fishers Station when he worked at the livery stable owned by Jim Gentry. For the last month, he had been working for the Lynn brothers, two miles south of town.

On the other side of the railroad tracks was another saloon owned by Hampton "Hamp" West. A farmer by occupation, he resided in Castleton. West was originally from North Carolina and had enlisted in the Confederate army. He was present for most of the major battles of the Civil War. He was at the Battle of Chancellorsville when General "Stonewall" Jackson was killed. He fought at Gettysburg during Bloody Pickett's charge, and during the Battle of Petersburg, he was struck in the face by shrapnel, which took off his left cheek, leaving his face partially disfigured. He was at Appomattox when General Lee surrendered. He didn't agree with the surrender, so West deserted. Knowing that he couldn't go back to the South, he traveled north with his brother until they settled in Castleton.

West had a reputation of being lazy and a not-so-good neighbor. Since opening up his saloon less than a year before, his reputation became worse. He was involved in a number of different altercations and was commonly known as a bully around town.

As rival saloon owners, there was no love lost between West and the Farrell brothers. Patrons had their favorite saloon, and they viewed the other saloon with disdain. Insulting the quality of each saloon's whiskey was a sure-fire way to start a fight.

George McCoy, a friend of Hamp West, entered the Farrell brothers' saloon. McCoy walked up to Adam Lynn and hurled an insult at him. Lynn threw a punch at McCoy, knocking him to the ground. He was then promptly thrown out of the saloon.

Within an hour, McCoy returned, this time accompanied by his friends, Bob Dawson and Hamp West. Dawson, in an attempt to avenge McCoy, attacked Adam Lynn. Dawson's punch signaled the fight was on, and this time the sides would be equally matched. It didn't take long before Dawson and McCoy were thrown out of the rear of the saloon, leaving Hamp West to defend himself.

While the Lynn brothers easily defeated McCoy and Dawson, West found himself matched up against Benjamin Fouch. As Fouch passed by West, he looked over his shoulder and asked West, "Who the hell are you?"

West responded that he was a friend of Dawson and McCoy. Adam Lynn interjected and said, "He is one of the God damn Wests, go for him."

According to West, Adam Lynn charged him and struck him in the head first. Fouch slipped on a pair of brass knuckles and landed a blow on West's temple at the same time that someone struck him with a hard object from behind. West fell to the floor, where he was kicked repeatedly. He took cover underneath the pool table.

They started to use pool sticks to get West out from underneath the pool table. Andy Farrell stepped in and promised West that if he would come out from underneath the pool table, they would not touch him. West took him at his word, and he slid from underneath the table.

As he stood up, Fouch told Andy to step aside because he had something he wanted to say to West. Apparently, what he wanted to say involved his fists and not words. Fouch, still wearing the brass knuckles, struck West in the head four times. The impact caused West to fall to the floor, and once again, he took refuge underneath the pool table.

They tried to pull him from underneath the table, but West maintained a death grip on the legs. Fouch got down on the ground and began to punch West repeatedly in the face before attempting to gouge his eyes out. After a few minutes, Fouch was pulled off of West. Someone opened up the front door, and West bolted out of the saloon as fast as he could.

Hamp West's face had been beaten to a bloody pulp. His clothes were torn and soaked with blood. Although his saloon was not that far from the Farrells' saloon, he thought that they might pursue him. So instead of taking the shortest direct route, he jumped a fence and stopped in the woods until he could no longer hear his pursuers. He washed most of the blood off in a nearby pond. Then he cut through Sarah Redwine's yard, past William Bolton's house and down an alley until he got back to his saloon.

As West entered his saloon, the patrons were in awe of his condition. McCoy and Dawson, who had already come back to the saloon, filled everyone in on the altercation they were just a party to. But no one, including McCoy and Dawson, were prepared for what they witnessed as West entered the saloon. West's patrons were extremely loyal, and they all wanted to go back to Farrell's and finish it. West, exhausted and beaten, urged them to forget it.

Meanwhile back at the Farrells' saloon, everyone was rejoicing at the victory, which was celebrated with more liquor. After a few games of pool and a lot more drinking, the decision was made to go have some more beers at Hamp West's saloon. It was a decision that would have dire consequences.

A small contingent of patrons from Farrell's saloon, which included the Lynn brothers and Fouch, started walking toward West's saloon. Hamp West saw them through the window and raced for the door to lock it. When the unwelcome guests tried to get in, West told them to go away. On three separate occasions, they were turned away.

On the last attempt, West noticed that Fouch had his right hand in his back pocket. In addition to having brass knuckles, Fouch, being a former deputy, was known to carry a revolver. West feared that he might try to shoot him through the door.

West had the door partially open as he was trying to convince them to leave his property. As he tried to close the door, the latch broke. He went to grab the keys from behind the bar. While he was away from the door, Dawson, apparently not afraid, opened up the door and invited them inside.

They strutted into the saloon as if they owned the place. West was already behind the bar as Fouch made his way toward him. With the brass knuckles still on his hand, he slammed his fist down hard on the bar and, staring West straight in the eye, proclaimed, "I am the best damned man in Mudsock and can whip any son of a bitch in it." He added that if anyone wanted to cut or shoot, he was available.

West was completely defeated, and he cowered at the sight of Fouch. He was still nursing his wounds from a short time earlier and didn't want any more trouble. According to West, he said that Fouch told him that he was there for a purpose. That purpose was to whip West and determine once and for all who the best man in Mudsock was. West tried to ask Fouch why he wanted to fight him.

Fouch responded, "Did you say that you were a better man than me?"

West answered, "Did I ever say such a thing?"

This exchange went on for a few minutes. Fouch then extended his hand to West, who refused to shake it. Fouch probably realized that West wouldn't shake his hand, so he used it as another way to threaten West. Fouch told West that he would receive another beating if he didn't shake his hand. West conceded defeat. He agreed to shake hands if it would make peace. He shook hands with Fouch, and then he shook hands with Adam Lynn.

If the handshake was not insulting enough, Adam Lynn told West that they deserved a round of drinks on the house. West refused. They said that if he served them drinks, they would go away and not disturb one thing in his saloon. West relented and agreed if it would make "peace and harmony."

After West poured them drinks, Fouch looked at West and said, "God damn you, you can't fight, and I can whip you on less ground than you are made." West's loyal supporters urged him to not be intimidated by Fouch, but West was doing everything he could to end it peacefully.

While Fouch and West were exchanging pleasantries, Dawson walked up to Daniel Lynn and put his arm around his neck. To some people, it would appear to be a form of affection between two friends. But the knife in Dawson's hand said otherwise.

Dawson, with a smirk on his face and his arm around Lynn's neck, said, "My dear boy, I knew your mother and I am going to kiss you for her." Insulting one's mother was almost as bad as insulting the quality of someone's whiskey.

The insult sent Daniel Lynn into a rage. He slipped out of Dawson's grasp and took a swing at him. The knife slipped in Dawson's hand, leaving a large gash. Before he had a chance to realize what happened, Fouch, who had been watching this unfold, punched Dawson in the head, dropping him to the ground.

Once Dawson fell to the ground, a general melee ensued. Twenty-five to thirty men began to fight one another using whatever weapons they had available. Pool balls were being thrown, cue sticks were broken over people's backs and axe handles were hurled through the air. People were scrambling to get out of the building as fast as they could.

There were conflicting stories of what happened when the melee ensued. Wesley Lynn stated that he pulled Fouch off of Dawson. As he was holding Fouch, Hamp West struck Fouch in the back of the head with a brass beer faucet. The blow knocked Fouch unconscious. As Wesley Lynn tried to pick him back up, he was struck in the back of the head. He dropped Fouch to the floor and ran out of the saloon.

Hamp West recalled the incident differently. Once the melee ensued, Adam Lynn ran toward West holding an axe. His swing missed the target, and West and Lynn found themselves locked together in a struggle. West was able to get free and grabbed a brass beer faucet and struck Adam Lynn. The impact was enough to convince Adam Lynn to get out of the saloon. As the Lynn brothers made their way to the door, West and Fouch found themselves on opposite ends of a table. As Fouch charged at him, West raised the beer faucet and struck Fouch on the front part of the head. Fouch immediately fell to the floor.

The saloon emptied pretty quickly, and everyone gathered outside. Most everyone had suffered some type of injury. West opened up the door of the saloon and shouted, "Some of you men had better come back here and get Fouch. Somebody's killed him."

"And you, Hamp West, you're the man that did it," shouted someone from the crowd.

The Lynn brothers went back into the saloon and carried out Fouch, who was still unconscious. Fouch was taken nearby to Tucker's drugstore to bandage up the wound on his head. He was then taken to the boardinghouse of Sarah Redwine. Her husband, James, was the victim of the first homicide in Fishers just six years before. As a widow, she opened up a boardinghouse to earn an income. Fouch was officially pronounced dead at 2:00 a.m.

Hamp West, badly injured, showed enough endurance that he walked home from his saloon. He added two extra miles to his route so that he could stop by the residence of R.E. Smith, a local attorney, to acquire his legal services. It wasn't until he got home that he received medical attention and it was revealed that he had a skull fracture and internal injuries.

While Fouch was dying, Andy Farrell had several altercations with his brother, Ed, throughout the night. Ed was commonly cited for drunkenness. The altercation stemmed from the role in the fracas that they had taken part in during the day. The brothers beat each other with whatever they could find in the saloon. After they had beaten themselves to exhaustion, they both passed out inside the saloon.

Early Sunday morning, the Hamilton County coroner arrived by train from Noblesville to hold an inquest into the death of Benjamin Fouch. The investigation started as soon as he arrived, but the town was by no means peaceful.

About the time that the coroner arrived in town, the Farrell brothers were waking up from their drunken stupor. They picked up right where they left off before they passed out. But this time, they would have others to contend with.

At around ten o'clock on Sunday morning, bartenders Elwood Hayworth and Thomas Pickens, friends of West, went to Farrell's saloon for a fight. They were met at the door by Andy Farrell holding a pair of revolvers. Realizing that they were outmatched, they fled. Andy pursued them, and shots rang out. Whatever quietness had settled over the town from the previous day's excitement was no longer. In a short time, the train depot was filled with residents wanting to know what was happening.

By noon, Hayworth and Pickens had returned, this time armed. As some people were gathering for church, a gunfight was underway in the center of town. Shots were exchanged between Andy and the belligerents. By 1:00 p.m., Hamilton County sheriff W.A Seamans, accompanied by a posse, had arrived from Noblesville to help restore order.

When the sheriff arrived in Fishers Station, Andy Farrell was patrolling the street in front of his saloon. He was bleeding profusely, and his clothes were torn and bloody. His hair and moustache were matted with coagulated blood. His face was unrecognizable. He attempted to resist the officers as they placed him under arrest. Some residents commented that he looked more like a wild animal than a human being. The liquor probably encouraged that.

The posse pursued Hayworth and Pickens. Pickens was arrested, but Hayworth was able to escape capture. A short time later, Pickens escaped custody. The sheriff had finally quelled the disturbance, and now the coroner could begin his investigation.

The inquest began on Sunday and concluded Wednesday evening. All of the witnesses interviewed, more than twenty, showed some signs of a beating: bruises, black eyes and bloody wounds. The investigation totaled seventy-eight pages. The examination of the body showed that Fouch had a skull fracture. The fracture extended from the right ear to a hole near the right temple. The source of the fracture was a large flesh wound on the top of the head. The coroner determined that Fouch had died from a severe blow to the head by a blunt object.

Hamp West was formally charged with the murder of Benjamin Fouch. Due to his extensive injuries, he was confined to his bed under guard by Frank Goddard, who had been deputized to watch him.

When Thomas Goodwin came to Fishers Station to preach, it wasn't just to preach about temperance. He felt that a negative impression of the town and its people needed rectifying. For, of all the participants of the two-day battle, not one was a resident of Fishers Station. They came from the country, Castleton and beyond. The residents were loving, respectful people who had no sympathies for the rioters who cast a dark shadow over the town.

A few days after the sermon, the grand jury of Hamilton County handed down eighteen indictments against various individuals for their involvement in the events that led to Fouch's death. But Hamp West was somehow spared. He was ordered to be released from custody, as the jury decided that West acted in self-defense. It wasn't a popular decision among the residents.

As for the saloons, the night of Fouch's death was the last day of operation for West's saloon. It was purchased a few months later by Michael Castetter, a well-respected Fishers resident, and it was turned into a harness shop.

The fate of the Farrell's saloon was a lot different. As the coroner inquest was wrapping up on Wednesday, the Farrell saloon caught fire sometime after midnight. The Farrell brothers were still feuding and happened to be in Indianapolis at the time of the fire. The saloon was a total loss. It was believed that during the fight, a stovepipe was knocked down, which led to the fire. However, there was great suspicion that it was arson.

January 1, 1882, ushered in a new year and was one of the quietest days the town had experienced in a long time. The residents rejoiced at the fact that there were no more saloons to tarnish the town's reputation. But that elation was short-lived, as two more saloons opened up the next month. While the residents had to contend with the saloons, they were grateful that no other incident as extreme as the one that occurred on November 19, 1881, ever happened again.

7
A WHITE CAP BEATING?

*White Caps to be enforced on you we understand that you are meserable mean to your wife we have organized for your benefiet and we will wate on you the first time we hear of you mistreating her we will just give you what you need one hundred lashes striped to the skin and will * * * you besides just as shure as the sun rises in the east. And if that won't dew we will double the dose on you and keep that in mind.*

—letter sent to Grant Gwinn, a farmer in Lapel, by the White Caps. The omitted part was too obscene for publication in 1889.

In large part due to the mass Irish and Scottish immigration to the United States, Halloween was becoming a mainstream holiday. It wasn't until the late nineteenth century that Halloween started to be celebrated coast to coast. Less than a week before Halloween 1892, the residents of Fishers woke up to a disturbing story that caused a ripple of fear throughout the community.

Henry Klepfer was the town drunk. He spent his time as a day laborer taking whatever odd jobs were available. At night, he could always be found at Underwood's saloon consuming his fair share of whiskey. It wasn't uncommon to see him stumbling home drunk. So when the residents of Fishers heard the story of what happened to Klepfer after he stumbled home from the bar, they didn't know whether it was true or something made up out of his drunken stupor. Had it not been for some residents who came to his aid, most of the community would have written it off as an elaborate story.

On Wednesday morning, October 26, 1892, Klepfer was found tied to a tree in his yard and beaten severely. Otis Castetter, who lived nearby, found Klepfer and released him from the chains that were binding him to the tree. With the assistance of a few more neighbors, they took Klepfer to Sam Kepner's blacksmith shop for medical attention. Kepner was one of the town's first marshals and well respected within the community. After his wounds were dressed and he was given a clean set of clothes, Klepfer disappeared to Indianapolis for a few days.

Fear throughout the community spread quickly once the story of what happened made its way back to Fishers. Shortly after arriving in Indianapolis, Klepfer told an amazing story of brutality and inhumanity that was picked up by newspapers across the country.

Klepfer admitted to coming home drunk and immediately passing out. Sometime around midnight, he was woken up by a group of masked assailants who broke into his house after kicking in the front door. There were about ten men, all wearing white masks. Klepfer was pulled out of his bed, and a rag was shoved into his mouth. Then he was carried outside, where he was tied to the tree with a chain and his arms and legs were bound with a clothesline.

The masked assailants took turns repeatedly beating Klepfer to the point where death seemed almost certain. He sustained multiple injuries, including a laceration on the side of his head that was almost three inches long. He eventually lost consciousness. His wife, Olive Klepfer, was also bound and gagged but not beaten. She was restrained so that she could not render aid to her husband. Just prior to losing consciousness, he remembered hearing the assailants singing, "I am soldier of the Cross."

Once he was released from the tree and received medical treatment, he escaped to Indianapolis for fear the assailants may return.

The residents of Fishers knew exactly who the masked assailants were—the White Caps. They resembled the Ku Klux Klan that formed in the southern states shortly after the Civil War. The White Caps wore white masks, rode in groups on horseback and engaged in lynchings and beatings. As much as they resembled the KKK, there were some major differences between the two organizations.

The White Caps were formed in southern Indiana during the 1880s just about the time that the first wave of the KKK was dying out in the South. While the KKK was focused primarily on the restoration of white supremacy, race was not a motivating factor for the White Caps. They were concerned primarily with violations of normalcy and anything that contributed to the decay of society. Irrespective of race or sex, the White Caps targeted those who were accused of being drunkards, adulterers, idlers, wife-beaters and any other offenses that the organization deemed detrimental to the good of society.

Their methods of enforcing the moral law of society were well known. Once an individual had been identified as a target, the White Caps would sometimes give a warning by leaving a sack of switches along with a note at the person's front door. The individual would have a few options: change and repent or leave town and never return. Failure to follow one of the options would result in a severe beating and sometimes death. Sometimes, depending on the offense, no warning would be given. Switches would sometimes be replaced with more violent means like bullets. It wasn't uncommon to burn down the house after a beating to make sure that the person left town.

Most attempts to prosecute White Cappers proved futile because the organization had members in positions in power within local and state governments.

It wasn't a surprise that Klepfer was beaten by the White Caps. A drunkard most of his life who occasionally beat his wife in his drunken state, his offenses were just what the White Caps were meant to enforce. What surprised the residents and made them fearful was that White Cap activity very rarely came that far north. While stories of White Cap atrocities dominated the local papers around the state, it was uncommon for them to operate outside of southern Indiana.

It had been three years since the last time there was White Cap activity in Hamilton County. Back in 1889, near the town of Sheridan, the White Caps took Stanton Hammock from his home and tied him to a tree. He was given twenty-five lashes and told to leave the state within twenty-four hours.

Hammock had been having an affair with Sarah Clampitt. Her husband, Mark Clampitt, suffered from severe mental issues and had been committed to various asylums for most of his life. While he was being treated in the asylum, she took up sexual relations with Hammock. Their relationship angered the community, and it wasn't long before the White Caps took matter into their own hands. After his severe beating, Hammock had the unique honor of being the only person in Hamilton County to have ever been whipped by the White Caps.

Just as fear that the White Caps had returned was spreading throughout the community, the residents were given another shock. Apparently, Klepfer fabricated the whole story of the White Cap beating to hide the fact that the beating was actually administered by his wife, Olive. His story began to unravel after his wife filed for divorce.

After Klepfer arrived home drunk that evening, he started to beat his wife with a butter churn and threw a chair at her. Some of his drinking buddies took him back to the bar for a few more drinks. When he arrived home again, Olive refused to let him inside. He was so drunk that he passed out next to the tree. She feared that he might force his way into the house, so she tied him to the tree with a chain and used a clothesline to tie his hands and legs.

Realizing he was tied to the tree, he swore obscenities at her and called her every vile name imaginable. Olive grabbed a switch, and every time he called her a name, she struck him. The beating finally aroused Castetter, who pleaded with her to let him go. Olive Klepfer said she feared her husband would kill her. Castetter rounded up a few more neighbors, and they promised to take Klepfer away and make sure he did not touch her. After he was cleaned up, they convinced him to leave town.

While Klepfer was telling the grand story about his White Cap beating, Olive was filing for divorce. A month later, it was official and Klepfer, already strapped for cash, had to pay her $300 in alimony.

Receiving a beating at the hands of his wife was not enough to deter him from the bottle. He continued to drink excessively. He had a few arrests for drunkenness and on at least one occasion was robbed when he was in his drunken state. He reported the robbery to the police, and although they were successful in locating the robbery suspect, Klepfer was also arrested for being drunk.

Henry Klepfer told an amazing tale about his beating at the hands of the White Caps. Perhaps he would have wished to have been beaten by them instead of his wife. The physical injuries he sustained paled in comparison to what the beating did to his pride. But if it did one thing, she made sure that he never beat another woman again.

8

THE MYSTERY OF THE ELLER BRIDGE ARSON

This is arson. The bridge could not have burned so quickly unless it had been saturated with an inflammable substance.
—Sheriff Ronald Guilkey, upon seeing the burning bridge

For close to a century, traversing the White River between Delaware and Clay Township required traveling across an iconic landmark, the Eller Bridge. This covered bridge spanning the width of the White River was one of the most picturesque places in all of central Indiana. Artists were drawn to the bridge for its inspiration and the natural beauty surrounding it. For others, it became a family outing destination. Parents wanted their children to experience the bridge just as they had when they were young. On October 5, 1957, the iconic bridge was destroyed by an arsonist in a crime that was never solved. Speculation still abounds, but it is a mystery that lives on.

When Hamilton County was first settled in 1818, the White River was a major natural obstacle, making any attempt to cross it a formidable task. Transportation across the river was limited to private boats or canoes. Then, in 1846, the county commissioners granted William Carlin the right to operate a ferry service. The ferry consisted of a flatboat that was large enough to hold one wagon and four horses. The ferry service was primitive. It used a series of ropes and pulleys attached on both sides of the river along with the natural currents to move the boat. An old canoe was used for those traveling by foot.

Passengers traveling by foot were charged five cents, while a man and one horse cost ten cents. For thirty-five cents, one could ferry a wagon and four horses. Livestock was charged two cents and one cent for each pig or sheep. Public servants were carried across at no charge.

For almost a quarter of a century, the ferry service was the primary transportation system—until Absolam Eller, who owned a majority of the land near the White River, petitioned the county commissioners for a bridge. In July 1869, Josiah Durfee was awarded the contract to construct the first bridge over the White River.

After a little more than a year, the Eller Bridge was finally completed at a cost of just under $13,000. For the first time along the twenty-mile route that the White River flows through Hamilton County, there was a permanent structure across the river. This wooden covered bridge spanning 311 feet above the river would for decades carry horses and carriages before giving way to automobiles. The bridge became a source of pride for the residents in this part of the county.

Longtime resident Myrtie Barker described the bridge eloquently:

> *It had a roof and boarded walls. Floorboards that rattled with every passing vehicle. Down below, the river flowed cool and clear. There were trees at the entrance to the bridge and along the little road that led up to the bridge. In summer, the leafy boughs made lacy shadows. And in winter the long limbs and branches and twigs wore white. The roof of the bridge was blanketed in snow, and at its eaves hung jagged icicles that glistened in the sun. Years ago the road bore the mark of wagon tracks. And inside the covered bridge the clop, clop, clop of horses' hoofs resounded with the rhythm of music.*

The Eller Bridge's design was known as a Howe truss bridge. It was one of the most popular bridge styles during the 1800s. It was economical due to the ease of construction and required little maintenance. The design of the bridge incorporated redundancy and flexibility, which allowed it to withstand excessive loading or the loss of a panel in the event of a collision. As automobiles replaced horse carriages, the bridge required little modifications to accommodate the added weight.

Because of the success of the Eller Bridge, Josiah Durfee was tasked with building a second bridge in Noblesville. Potter's Bridge was completed less than a year later and opened to traffic on April 11, 1871. The construction cost and style were the same as the Eller Bridge. Now that Hamilton County had two bridges, the ferry system was discontinued.

Eller Bridge. *Larry A. Reynolds.*

At the turn of the century, more bridges began to appear across the White River. And by the 1950s, Hamilton County boasted eight bridges, but the days of the covered bridge were over. Beginning in the 1890s, steel was in abundance, and iron bridges became the norm like the Riverwood and Strawtown Bridge in the northern part of Hamilton County. That would give way to concrete bridges such as the Connor Street Bridge in Noblesville and the one-lane John Owens Bridge (146th Street), named for one of Noblesville's postmasters.

The Eller Bridge became somewhat of a symbol of the divide between Delaware and Clay Townships. In the 1950s, petitions had started to circulate in an attempt to redraw the township lines. The issue of schools became a politically charged subject, and some residents wanted the part of Delaware Township that was west of the river to be merged with Clay Township and use the White River, a natural feature, as the dividing line. (See "The Great School Controversy," chapter 11, for more information.)

Because of the rising tensions, the Eller Bridge became the scene of a few arson attempts. Whether it was teenage pranks or something more sinister would remain a mystery. However, burning the bridge would send a strong statement in support of dividing Delaware Township at the White River.

The first arson attempt came in 1953. Several gallons of gasoline were poured onto the wooden floor of the bridge. The arsonist started the fire on the roadway, and the fire followed the trail of gasoline, igniting the bridge. By a sheer miracle, two motorists came upon the fire at almost exactly the same time and extinguished it before the flames could do any damage. Although there were no suspects, a gallon jar of gasoline hidden in the weeds was found near the bridge. Fire investigators determined that approximately three to four gallons of gasoline had been used to soak the floor of the bridge. The arsonists were never found.

Another attempt was made in 1955, but the bridge would remain intact with only a few charred timbers.

On Saturday, October 5, 1957, the first alarm sounded at about 9:30 p.m. in the Carmel firehouse. Within ten minutes, the first firetruck arrived to witness a towering inferno. The Eller Bridge was totally consumed by fire. Flames were shooting seventy-five to one hundred feet in the air. Noblesville and Fishers fire departments were also called to the scene to battle the blaze from the other side of the river. Fishers had just recently formed its own fire department instead of using Carmel's fire department. High winds forced the firefighters to fight the blaze from a distance. Within minutes, the bridge crashed thirty feet into the White River.

There were a few eyewitnesses. One witness reported seeing an individual on the bridge holding a flashlight shortly before 9:30 p.m. Another witness, who initially reported the incident, was sitting outside in the back of their home and noticed that the fire lit up the night sky. Sheriff Ronald Guilkey was adamant that it was arson. It was estimated that the bridge collapsed within fifteen minutes of the fire being first reported.

The next day, the state fire marshal inspected the structure. After four thousand gallons of water were poured onto the fire, the structure was still burning twenty-four hours later. Ironically, the fire started on the eve of Fire Prevention Week. With little physical evidence and no eyewitnesses to make a positive identification, it would become another unsolved arson.

Once the realization set in that the Eller Bridge, which had stood for eighty-eight years, was resting at the bottom of the river, the focus was how to replace it. It was not going to be an easy task.

Hamilton County was already facing staggering financial problems. The estimated cost to repair the bridge was $650,000 to $750,000. That amount was twice the total budget for Hamilton County in one year. Repairing the bridge would cost more than it cost to build Riverview Hospital.

Replacing the bridge was a major priority. It was a vital transportation link for the entire county. It was an essential route for schools. There were students in Delaware Township who attended Carmel schools, and being able to get to school would become a major obstacle. New housing additions would be put on hold, and recreational areas such as Northern Beach faced the prospect of going out of business.

The destruction of the Eller Bridge magnified the inadequacies of other bridges in Hamilton County. The nearest bridge, the John Owens Bridge (present-day 146th Street), was a one-lane bridge that had not been properly maintained. The Owens bridge would not be able to handle the increased traffic. A temporary bridge over the White River was ruled out because it would not hold up and would only increase the cost to the taxpayers.

When the Eller Bridge was first constructed, it was built at an angle with sharp curves at both ends. Plans were made to eliminate the curves and straighten the bridge to make travel safer. Hamilton County received a blessing when the federal government agreed to finance 50 percent of the project. That left the taxpayers with a price tag of $265,000.

It took almost two years for the new bridge to be completed. The project began on March 16, 1959, and it opened to traffic five months later. The

Eller Bridge showing the sharp curve that was straightened when the new bridge was built. *Larry A. Reynolds.*

Eller Bridge, 1940s to present day. *Larry A. Reynolds and author's collection.*

new reinforced concrete girder bridge would extend 613 feet across the White River and once again reconnect Delaware and Clay Townships.

Author's Note

In researching this chapter, the author came across information that the arson was a teenage prank gone wrong. The individuals responsible have kept it quiet for sixty-three years. Although the statutes of limitations have passed, their identities will remain a secret.

9

THE CITY UNDER THE LAKE

That project ruined a wonderful little village. We all got along fine there.
—Fred Martin, Germantown resident

Geist Reservoir is a popular boating and fishing destination straddling the Marion and Hamilton County line. Surrounded by multimillion-dollar homes, the lake has become a haven for the ultrawealthy. But ten feet below the water, the lake holds a secret: an abandoned town whose only remnants are building foundations buried below.

Its name was Germantown, not to be confused with East Germantown in Wayne County, near the Ohio state line. The town was first laid out on March 1, 1834, by the Beaver brothers, John, Solomon and George. It was the oldest town in Lawrence Township located within Marion County.

Prior to being submerged under ten feet of water, Germantown sat on the north bank of Fall Creek. This waterway flows fifty-seven and a half miles beginning in Henry County, meandering its way through Madison and Hamilton Counties before emptying into the White River in downtown Indianapolis.

Originally, the only way to get across Fall Creek was a swinging foot bridge. Most of the children had to cross the river in order to get to school, which was located a mile from town. Wagons had to cross the creek at its lowest point. In the winter, the creek would freeze so solidly that wagons could easily traverse the icy surface. In 1901, the footbridge was eventually replaced by a wagon bridge that would serve both vehicles and people.

The post office in Germantown was established on April 24, 1837, with Samuel Cunningham as its first postmaster. The town began to flourish, and eventually it had a general store, a blacksmith shop, a shoe repair shop and flour and sawmills. There were about twenty homes that made up Germantown, with half in Marion County and the other half in Hamilton County. Germantown lost its post office in 1870, when it was moved to the nearby town of Oaklandon. The railroad had just been built through the town, and residents were forced to travel to receive their mail until the rural mail carrier route was established.

Life in Germantown was like most any other small town. Everyone in the community depended on one another, and they took pride in their town. But beginning in the 1920s, the residents started noticing their peaceful village might be no more. And it all began with a water study in 1923.

The Indianapolis Water Company, created in 1881, and its predecessor, the Water Works Company of Indianapolis, was established at a time when utilities were privately owned. Those who ran the company were prominent people in the community, and three of them went on to be governors of Indiana.

In 1913, the Indianapolis Water Company was purchased by Clarence Geist, the lake's namesake. Geist, having been born in La Porte, Indiana, was a Philadelphia utilities magnate and one of the wealthiest and influential people in the United States. At the time he purchased the Indianapolis Water Company, the company was considered the largest privately owned water utility in the country. More than one hundred different utility companies fell under his control, with assets totaling over $50 million.

Clarence Geist, president of the Indianapolis Water Company. Geist Reservoir is named in his honor. *From the* Indianapolis Star.

Clarence Geist was not greeted warmly in Indianapolis upon his purchase of the company. The previous owners, Linnaes Boyd and Hugh Landon, were Indianapolis natives and well respected. Geist was an outsider who didn't even live in Indiana. Four months after the purchase of the company, Indiana passed the Public Utility Law, which specified that most of the board of directors and all officers of a utility must reside in Indiana. Geist stepped down as president and instead assumed the newly created position of chairman of the board to sidestep the new law.

As soon as Geist took over the company, one of the first moves he made was hiring Leonard Metcalf as a water company consultant. Metcalf came from the prestigious engineering company Metcalf and Eddy out of Boston, Massachusetts. He was known as the country's most respected hydraulic engineer.

One of his first assignments was to compile a report on the future water needs of Indianapolis. In 1923, that report was submitted to the water company. It forecasted that the natural supply of water from White River and Fall Creek would be insufficient for the projected growth of Indianapolis. The recommendation was to create a reservoir on Fall Creek that would address the city's future water needs.

Clarence Geist immediately began to address the concerns raised by the Metcalf study. In 1924, meterization began reducing water usage among the residents, and it continued until 1932, as the United States was dealing with the effects of the Great Depression.

Beginning in 1928, Germantown residents started coming to the realization that the new reservoir would probably consume their town. The Indianapolis Water Company began buying land all around them in readiness for the new reservoir. Through the 1930s, the water company bought 5,455 acres of land at a cost of $350 an acre. Some 1,800 acres were designated as water surface, while the rest of the acreage was for land needed for pollution control.

The residents seemed to take it in stride and realized there wasn't much use to fight it. The residents sold out to the Indianapolis Water Company. The buildings were dismantled, and it marked the end of Germantown. It appears that the only complaint that the residents had was that the reservoir was not named Germantown.

Instead, the reservoir was named after Clarence Geist. However, he did not live long enough to see it through to its construction. Geist died at the age of sixty-four on Sunday, June 12, 1938, at his home in Villanova, Pennsylvania. He left behind an $11 million estate to his widow and three children.

Back in Indianapolis, the death of Geist hardly affected the operation of the water company. That was mostly due to Howard Scott Morse, who had been the general manager of the water company since 1925. Nicknamed "Mr. Water Company," he was very popular in Indianapolis.

It was Morse who oversaw the construction of the new reservoir. In April 1941, the Indiana Public Service Commission gave authorization for the Indianapolis Water Company to proceed with the construction of the reservoir. The contract was awarded to the Indianapolis construction firm Smith and Johnson. Their bid of $627,245 was the lowest of the eight submitted. The plans called for the 7.5-mile lake to cover over 2,000 acres of land with the dam being 30 feet high and 1,800 feet long.

Construction began in May 1941. The project couldn't have started at a better time, for Indianapolis was experiencing its worst drought in fifty years. For the previous ten years, there had been a deficiency of rainfall amounting to ten inches, which led to lower water levels.

Construction was finally completed at a cost of over $2.5 million. The reservoir was filled to capacity for the first time in March 1943. The newly created seven-billion-gallon reservoir gave Indianapolis a major water source to meet the demands of a growing city. The new lake covered more than two thousand acres of land in Marion, Hamilton and Hancock Counties. At the time of its construction, only two other lakes in Indiana were bigger, Wawasee and Maxinkuckee, both natural lakes.

After the reservoir's completion, Scotty Morse was concerned about human contamination of the water supply. He prohibited swimming, boating and fishing on Geist, which angered the avid sportsmen of the area. In 1947, the Indiana Department of Conservation considered making Geist a state park. As an alternative, Morse opened a section of the lake for fishing, and it became an instant success.

The 1950s saw more recreational opportunities on Geist. In 1950, the first subdivision, Luxhaven, was built at the mouth of Geist. The twenty-six acres of land would house 116 cabins priced from $500 to $1,000 each. Summers had become so popular on Geist, with crowds numbering into the thousands, that the county commissioners invoked parking restrictions. In 1955, the Indianapolis Sailing Club signed a ten-year lease, and boating on Geist had become a reality.

Morse, who didn't want the water contaminated, had deemed the land around the lake "unfit" to farm or live on. This unfit land was sold to the water company for pennies of what it was worth. It was then turned around and sold for exorbitant prices for new home construction beginning in the 1970s. Home prices have skyrocketed since the first cabins were built in Luxhaven, with homes priced in the millions of dollars.

Scotty Morse, who helped make the Geist Reservoir a reality, also got a reservoir named after him. Morse Reservoir, located in the northern part of Hamilton County, was completed in 1956.

All that remains of Germantown are building foundations. Most of the lumber found its way to Fortville, which was used to build some homes and a grain elevator. Tourists and residents flock to Geist every year, but very few know what lies beneath the surface.

10
THE GRAVE ROBBING TRIALS OF 1903

I have robbed graves so long that I overcame any scruples that I felt long ago. It was a matter of business.
—*Rufus Cantrell*

What does a medical school, multiple prominent physicians and a gang of grave robbers have in common? They would all come together to create one of the biggest scandals ever seen in this part of the country. Two Indianapolis police detectives would unravel a criminal enterprise of multiple gangs of grave robbers dating years back. The investigation would lead to the discovery of wholesale desecration of multiple graveyards in Marion and surrounding counties, all at the behest of a well-known medical school. It also shed light on a three-year-old cold case of a missing woman. The scandal engulfed the small town of Fishers, which would have its own sensational trial in Noblesville.

And it all started with an anonymous tip.

Stella Middleton was only sixteen years old when she died. A Black woman, she lived in the Irvington neighborhood, a suburb of Indianapolis. Irvington is five miles from downtown Indianapolis and was the home of Butler University until it moved in 1928. Her death, in August 1902, came as a shock to many, as she showed no signs of being sick. She was buried in the Anderson cemetery between the Irvington and Brightwood neighborhoods.

Stella's mother, still grieving from her daughter's death, arrived home on the night of September 17 after attending a prayer meeting at her church.

She discovered a note on her door. The note read that the body of her daughter had been removed from its final resting place, and it could be found at the Central College of Physicians and Surgeons in downtown Indianapolis. The letter was unsigned, and her first thought was to disregard it as a sick joke. After consulting with family members, she went to court, and Justice William Nickerson, solely on the basis of the anonymous note, issued a search warrant to look for the body at the medical school.

The Central College of Physicians and Surgeons, established in 1879, was a training school for white doctors. It was located at the corner of Pennsylvania and South Streets. A new building was under construction at 212 North Senate Avenue, directly across the street from the statehouse. This new four-story medical school, with its dissecting rooms, back alleys and large basement with vaults would become synonymous with the illegal practice of grave robbing.

The mother of Stella Middleton, accompanied by several relatives and a constable, arrived at the college to execute the search warrant. After a brief search, they discovered multiple bodies lying on dissection tables. Mrs. Middleton identified one of the bodies as that of her daughter, Stella. She stayed with her daughter until the body was picked up. Her daughter was reburied the next day, and to ensure her body would remain undisturbed, heavy boards were placed on the coffin.

Samuel S. Gerber, captain of the detectives of the Indianapolis Police Department. *From the* Indianapolis News.

On the same night that Mrs. Middleton received her anonymous note, another Irvington resident, Wesley Gates, was approached by a dark figure in a horse carriage. Unable to make out the face of the stranger, he heard a muffled voice tell him that his daughter, Glendore Gates, had been stolen from the Anderson cemetery and the body could be found at the Central College. The next day, he dug up the grave of his daughter and noticed that the canvas cloth that was sewn onto the coffin was still intact. He assumed that his daughter's body had not been taken, but he noticed many other graves that had been tampered with.

Upon discovery of the body of Stella Middleton at the college and the grave tampering, Mrs. Middleton and Mr. Gates called upon Captain Samuel Gerber, chief of the detectives of the Indianapolis Police Department. Two detectives were immediately assigned to investigate the case, Chauncey Manning and Adolph Asch.

Chauncey Manning was a rookie in the detective division. He joined the Indianapolis Police Department in 1898 and was promoted to detective because of his impressive interrogation skills. He had been a detective for only about six months before he was assigned the case. This Indiana native was young, clean shaven and a stark contrast to his partner.

Adolph Asch, fourteen years Manning's senior, was a veteran officer. He joined the police department in 1888 and was promoted to detective in 1897. He was born in Alsace-Lorraine while it was under French control, before Germany annexed it following victory in the Franco-Prussian War. Unlike Manning, he was a European immigrant, older, with a thick, bushy moustache. He was fluent in English, German, French and Italian, which made him invaluable as an interpreter. Asch's other skill was his attention to detail. He also exhibited a work ethic that not many could match. He would refuse to stop working for lunch or dinner, and other detectives would pull straws to avoid being assigned as his partner. Being the rookie detective, Manning was the odd man out. But their work on this case would lead to a long career together.

The detectives started their investigation by meeting with the dean of the college, Dr. Allison Maxwell. He admitted knowing that the body of Stella Middleton was there, but he did not know how it got there. The detectives were informed that the bodies were acquired through Dr. Joseph C. Alexander, the demonstrator of anatomy at the college. He provided the college with bodies for dissecting purposes. Whether it was intentional or by accident, Dr. Maxwell told the detectives something that would break the case wide open. He said that the body was brought to the school by a Black man whom Dr. Alexander paid.

It wasn't long before the detectives identified the mysterious man as Rufus Cantrell. Cantrell was no stranger to the police. At the age of sixteen, he moved to Indianapolis with his mother from Gallatin, Tennessee. As a young kid, he could recite whole passages of the Bible and believed that he could talk to God. Upon arrival in Indianapolis, he tried to become a teenage preacher, holding sermons in the streets. His sermons could turn profane, and that is when Cantrell's true colors would show.

Cantrell would never back down from a fight, no matter how trivial. In 1900, he started a bar fight over his support for Democratic presidential candidate William Jennings Bryan. In 1901, he got into a fight that ended with Cantrell shooting a man in the forehead, but somehow causing only

Adolph Asch, promoted to captain of detectives, 1906. *Indianapolis Public Library*.

minor injury. Cantrell was also a witness to the murder of Indianapolis merchant police officer John Watterson, in 1893. Watterson was stoned to death as he tried to break up a burglary at Gilman & Carney's meat market. There was much speculation that Cantrell murdered the officer. The officer's murder was never solved.

As good as Manning was at interrogating suspects, neither he nor Asch were prepared for the confession that Cantrell would give. Realizing he had been caught and in an attempt to get leniency, he made a full confession and admitted to being the leader of a gang of grave robbers, commonly referred to as "ghouls." Their group was known as the "Sign of the Cross," which was derived from the way that members would sign letters detailing murders. In the previous three months, hundreds of graves had been emptied from various cemeteries in Indianapolis, including Crown Hill and Mount Jackson. As soon as a body was buried in Mount Jackson, it was dug up. Cantrell said, "I don't believe that we have missed anybody that's been placed there since July."

On Sunday, September 28, Cantrell and six others were formally arrested for grave robbing. The other six defendants, Isom Donnell, William Jones,

Buford Cooley, Walter Daniels, Sol Grady and Samuel Martin, all confessed and corroborated Cantrell's story. Most of them had been in the business of grave robbing for several years, and they demonstrated how they did it.

They would make note of any funerals in the area. After making mental notes of the locations of the freshly buried bodies, they would come back in the dark of the night. They used a three-seated wagon with a canopy and side curtains, which contained all of their tools. With a group of between four and seven men, they would open up multiple graves at the same time. Two men would open up the grave and remove the body. The grave then would be refilled as if nothing was disturbed. Cantrell made it into an art form by digging down into the center of the grave instead of the head. They would saw through the coffin and push back the small lid and then slide the body out. The only light used was an occasional match. Any jewelry on the body was kept by the men who dug up the grave.

Cantrell bragged that the grave robbing of Glendore Gates was his best yet. He noticed that there was a canvas over the pine box. In order to get the body, he had to rip the canvas. He took the extra time to sew the canvas back up before filling in the grave. When Gates's father opened up the grave and noted the canvas was intact, he assumed the body was still in there. However, his daughter had been taken to the Central College. Cantrell even took the time to put the flowers back on the grave.

All of the ghouls implicated Dr. Joseph Alexander as the mastermind behind the grave robbing. He had occasionally accompanied the ghouls on many of their expeditions. For the most part, Alexander and Cantrell would travel around the city making a list of what graves to rob. The ghouls had become so proficient that it would take only about twenty-five minutes to rob a grave. After the bodies were removed, they were transported to the Central College. Upon the ghouls uttering the password, *Rufus*, the doors opened and the body would be dropped off. They were paid $30 for each body. Based on the confessions, Dr. Alexander was arrested the next day and released on a $2,000 bond.

Dr. Alexander was originally from Fishers. He taught school for a number of years in Fishers before leaving to attend medical school. In 1895, he graduated from the Indiana Medical College with honors. He had become a favorite son to the residents of Fishers because of his success and often returned to visit his family.

Although Dr. Alexander proclaimed his innocence and firmly stated that he didn't know Cantrell or any of his accomplices, the detectives found damaging evidence to the contrary. Just by chance, a local gunsmith, Gus

Habich, went to the police station because he had not been paid for some shotguns. He told the detectives that a group of Black men had come to his store to buy some shotguns on credit and Dr. Alexander was the signer for that credit. Cantrell's gang was usually always armed when they robbed graves. When the grave robbing incident hit the news, the ghouls became scared and pawned the shotguns at a store near the statehouse. Dr. Alexander denied any knowledge of this, but public opinion was turning against him.

As the scandal began to unravel, suspicions started to arise about who was the anonymous tipster. A note was left for Mrs. Middleton, a strange figure approached Mr. Gates and it was discovered later that the husband of Rose Neidlinger received a phone call that his wife's body was removed. It was found at the Central College in a pickling barrel. Some accused Rufus Cantrell of being the tipster; others thought it might be jealousy between ghouls in the awarding of "contracts" with other medical schools or it could have been a faculty member at the college.

Another search warrant was conducted at the college for Glendore Gates. The search was quick, as there was only one body. The detectives thought that was odd considering just a week prior when the body of Rose Niedlinger was discovered, there was eight bodies. The college was in the process of moving into a new building on Senate Avenue. Although it was still under construction, it was believed that the bodies had been moved to the new location. The detectives found nothing, and the body of Mrs. Gates remained a mystery.

On October 1, a large gathering of white and Black spectators packed the courtroom to see the first court hearing of the grave robbing trial and catch a glimpse of the defendants. William P. Herrod, attorney for Dr. Alexander, requested a continuance until October 23. Amid the sighs of disappointment of no trial, the defendants filed out of the courtroom. As the ghouls were led out, a large gathering of Black spectators expressed how they felt about the defendants. The ghouls had brought disgrace upon their race. But they left the majority of their disgust for Dr. Alexander, for had it not been for him, the ghouls would not have done what they did.

Marion County prosecutor John C. Ruckelshaus vowed that no person was above the law, and regardless of race, each person associated with grave robbing would be held accountable to the fullest extent of the law. A grand jury was convened for October 13. The law was clear. Every medical college must keep a record of all bodies taken for dissection, and it could be seen by anyone on demand. It must list the name and address of who delivered the body and how much was paid for it. Violations were a fine between $100 and $500 and one to five years in the county jail. If a body, of which there was no record, was dissected, it was a felony punishable by one to three years. Based on this law, four other physicians would also be indicted.

Rufus Cantrell began to enjoy his new-found publicity. Every day, he accompanied Detectives Asch and Manning around the city in the search of graves that he robbed and the searches of the medical schools for the bodies. He became so comfortable with them that he was given the occasional cigar. Cantrell loved to talk about his exploits. When he was a preacher for a small church in Indianapolis, he presided over the funerals of parishioners. While he was preaching, he would already be figuring out when to take the body. As if it was a joke, he laughed when he recalled stealing a body before the funeral. The undertaker, who assisted in the scheme, let Cantrell take the body, and the coffin contained only a pack of playing cards. Cantrell acted as a pallbearer knowing that coffin was empty.

The mystery of Glendore Gates was finally solved. On October 17, a resident was walking to work, and as he passed the Central College, he noticed four sacks near the rear door to the college. One of the sacks was sitting upright. Figuring that the sacks contained bodies, he notified the police. The bodies of Gates and four other individuals that the detectives had been searching for were recovered.

On October 25, the grand jury returned twenty-five indictments against the ghouls, five physicians, several undertakers and custodians of various cemeteries.

HAMILTON COUNTY

Cantrell maintained that theirs was not the only group engaged in the grave robbing business. Cemeteries were divided into territories, which were under the control of one or more ghouls. Robbing a grave within someone else's territory required permission and a cut of the fee.

Graving robbing was big business in Hamilton County. Body snatching had been going on for at least seven years. Local ghouls would steal the bodies and then leave them in designated areas for Cantrell, who would then transport them to the medical colleges. Cantrell acted as the go-between, and the money would be split between the two of them. According to Cantrell, of all the cities and counties he worked in, he knew of more bodies taken from Hamilton County than any other.

The southern part of Hamilton County was under the control of Wade Hampton "Hamp" West. West was an infamous character in Fishers. He was once a saloonkeeper, famously known as the man who killed Benjamin Fouch back in 1881 with a beer faucet to prove who was "the best damn man in Mudsock." He was acquitted of murder by reason of self-defense. His saloon closed after he was arrested, and after his acquittal, he went back to farming.

While Hampton West controlled many of the cemeteries in the southern part of Hamilton County, he was assisted by a wealthy farmer who lived on the other side of the county. Lucius Stout lived in Eagletown, near Westfield, and he would supply West with information on burials of people who died in his neighborhood. They used the codenames Parker and Sullivan for Hamp West and Lucius Stout, respectively.

Cantrell told the detectives a lavish tale of grave robbing and murder that occurred almost two years before. In September 1901, Cantrell and four members of his gang showed up at the Beaver Cemetery (today Highland Cemetery) in an undeveloped part of Fishers. As they were removing a body from the grave, West and Stout showed up and ordered them away from the grave, as they didn't have permission. This wasn't the first time that Cantrell's gang had a run-in with West.

Cantrell refused to leave without the body. In a show of force, West and Stout drew their revolvers, and being at a disadvantage, Cantrell's gang fled. Shots were exchanged. One of Stout's shots struck William Gray, a thirty-eight-year-old white man from Johnston County, who had accompanied Cantrell on numerous expeditions. West also took a round in the leg, which gave him a pronounced limp in the weeks after.

The gang fled the area, leaving William Gray behind. They never saw him again. Cantrell testified that West took the wounded ghoul to his farm, where he died. The next day, West and Stout disposed of the body in the Fall Creek swamp. West and Stout would later testify that Gray fled to Wheeling, West Virginia, but there was no evidence to back up that assertion. Attempts to search the creek for the body proved fruitless.

The corpse, Newton Bracken, showed up at the Central College the next evening transported by West and Stout, who were expecting to be paid. When Cantrell told Dr. Alexander that his group was responsible for lifting the body, Cantrell was the one who walked away with the money.

Based on the information, the detectives arrested West in the early part of December and charged him with two counts of grave robbing in criminal court in Marion County. With these new revelations of grave robbing, the Hamilton County Sheriff's Office launched its own investigation.

Just days into the new year, 1903, Hamilton County sheriff Albert Fox made his first arrest of Hamp West. He was charged with two more counts of grave robbing. West was charged with the theft of Newton Bracken in September and disturbing the grave of Walter Manship, who died in January 1901. West was already out on bond on the charges in Marion County, and he was taken to Noblesville to post bond for the two new charges.

The company that posted West's bond in Marion County refused to post his bond in Hamilton County. It had already posted $5,000 and refused to take on anymore liability. West came to the realization that he might be in jail for a long time.

Intense hatred of Hamp West could be felt all over town. West never had a good reputation among the residents, and the bar brawl in 1881 brought the town unwanted publicity. Now the residents were dealing with another incident that was much worse. West was accused of robbing the grave of his own niece, Ida West. His brother John, who lived in Fishers, buried his daughter, and the funeral was attended by all the relatives and many of the Fishers residents. West had a habit of attending every funeral in the area. The next day after the funeral of Ida West, Hamp enlisted the help of John Morgan, who lived nearby, to help him locate the grave. There was no headstone, just a few mounds of dirt. He pretended that he wanted to lay some flowers on the grave, but later, when the coffin was opened, the body was gone.

Shortly after his arrest in Marion County, West bought a house in Fishers Station. At the time, he lived about two miles outside of town. Before he could move into the house, someone burned it to the ground. A few days later, he leased another house and moved in during the night. He soon enlisted the help of a carpenter to do some work on the house. But the following day, residents pressured the carpenter to quit. The residents were making it clear how they felt about Hamp West.

As the trial of Dr. Alexander was about to get underway, a group of detectives were dispatched to Hamilton County to assist the sheriff in identifying all those who might be involved in grave robbing. As horrifying as the details were that came out from Indianapolis, it was alleged that Hamilton County was operating on a much larger scale, and upward of one thousand bodies had been stolen in the last few years.

Trial of Dr. Alexander

Dr. Alexander went on trial on Monday, February 2, 1903. Alexander would be the first one to go on trial out of the thirty-nine people under indictment. There had never been a criminal case in the state of Indiana as sensational as the trial of Alexander. Every day of the trial, the courtroom was packed with over five hundred spectators, mostly women, who would stay and listen until the end of the day.

The prosecution was headed by Prosecutor Ruckelshaus and assisted by deputy prosecutor Charles Benedict and William T. Brown. Alexander had an all-star defense team whose legal fees were paid for by the college. His defense was led by Henry N. Spaan and assisted by William P. Herod, Joseph B. Kealing and Martin Hugg. On a motion by the defense, Judge Alford appointed a special judge, John M. Bailey, to hear the case.

The prosecution started its case by calling Mason Neidlinger, whose wife was found at the Central College. The star witness, Rufus Cantrell, would follow. His testimony wasn't planned to be earth-shattering, as it basically followed the script of what he had already told the detectives. But he dropped a bombshell that would surprise even the other ghouls.

Cantrell testified that he was romantically involved with Stella Middleton. He went out of town for a short period, and when he returned, he discovered that she died while he was away. He was unsure of where she was actually buried in the Anderson cemetery. A group of ghouls, including Cantrell, were in the process of stealing a body. When they arrived at the Central College, Cantrell was shocked to see that the body was that of Stella. Cantrell became emotional, but he had to conceal it from the other ghouls. Cantrell was struck with so much guilt that he confessed that he was the informant. He left the note for Mrs. Middleton and then contacted Mr. Gates and Mr. Neidlinger. Everyone in the courtroom was astonished.

The state would eventually call six of the ghouls to testify that they had either met Dr. Alexander, been paid by him or that he had accompanied them on several grave-robbing expeditions. Three witnesses who were employed by the livery stable also testified. They said that Dr. Alexander, along with Cantrell, rented horses, and all the bills were paid by the doctor.

Justice of the peace for Center Township W.H. Nickerson testified that he issued the search warrant and accompanied Mrs. Middleton to the Central College, where they discovered the body of her daughter lying on a table. But perhaps the most damaging testimony was when the state submitted into evidence a silk shroud that was worn by Catherine Doehring when she was buried. The witness, William Patty, testified that the silk shroud was discovered in the cellar of the college. As the jury was leaning forward to hear the details, Dr. Alexander was completely motionless.

John C. Ruckelshaus, Marion County prosecutor. *Public domain.*

The defense of Dr. Alexander started off in a most unusual way. Henry Spaan's opening statement took three hours. The opening statement went on for so long that the prosecution objected twice. Judge Bailey overruled the objection, asserting that Spaan was within the professional standards of the profession. Ruckelshaus showed his arrogance when he asked Judge Bailey for a definition of an opening statement. He was politely ignored.

Since the opening statement took up the entire morning, the defense was ready to present its case that afternoon. Alexander's defense team tried to discredit Cantrell's testimony by calling into question his character and his criminal record. They would argue that Cantrell could not tell the truth and that his testimony should not be considered.

Dr. Joseph Alexander. *From the* Indianapolis News, *September 29, 1902.*

Cantrell's criminal history was presented to the jury. From the age of fifteen to 1903, he was in and out of jail. He was an iterant preacher and would lead prayer meetings at the Marion County jail. While he alternated preaching and then robbing the graves he presided over, he also engaged in embezzlement. He stole from the Mount Zion Baptist Church, which employed him as a preacher. He had no shame or regrets and was mostly an alcoholic. He deserted his wife and child and admitted to an affair in open court. The defense maintained that Cantrell was proud of his criminal acts and expressed no remorse.

The defense didn't stop there. In addition to his criminal history, Cantrell's sanity was brought before the jury. The defense called three medical experts to testify that Cantrell was legally insane. Dr. Ernest Reyer was a doctor with the state hospital for the insane. On cross-examination, he described Cantrell as "morally insane from birth yet intellectually able and capable of remembering and describing events accurately." That was the opposite of what the defense was going for.

Two other doctors, Dr. W.B. Fletcher and Dr. William Charles White, testified that Cantrell was insane. Fletcher was a specialist on nerve and brain diseases, and White was a professor of pathology. The prosecution would try to discredit their testimony by their association with the Central College. Fletcher was a doctor with the college for eight years, and White was the current chair of the pathology department at the college. Their bias was called into question.

Cantrell's military record would be submitted into evidence in support of his insanity. Cantrell enlisted in the army in 1897 and was assigned to Company A of the Twenty-Fourth Infantry Regiment. He was discharged from the army at Fort Douglas, Utah, soon after enlisting. The surgeon's certificate for discharge stated "disability from epilepsy, followed by confusional and suicidal inclinations existing prior to his entry into the United States service."

The defense would call fourteen witnesses to testify to the character of Dr. Alexander. The list was a collection of doctors, druggists, former deputy prosecutors and even a city council member, Crall Heard, who posted the bond for Dr. Alexander.

After ten days, both the prosecution and the defense rested, and the case rested in the hands of the jury. The last day of the trial, Friday, February 13, 1903, turned out to produce the most dramatic moment of the entire trial. As the jury was receiving instructions from the judge, Frank Doehring, son of Katherine Doehring, yelled out in the courtroom that if the jury should fail to convict, he would take the law into his own hands and send a bullet into the doctor's brain. John Neidlinger, husband of Rose Neidlinger, pointed a finger at Dr. Alexander and declared that if the jury failed to punish him, he would see that the penalty was paid.

The jury deliberated for fourteen hours and was unable to reach a verdict. The jury was sequestered for the weekend. Because of the threats made in the courtroom, two private detectives stood guard at the residence of Dr. Alexander. He barely slept and paced the floor throughout the night.

There was great anticipation among everyone in the courtroom as the jury went back to deliberating. But as the day wore on, anticipation turned into concern. At the end of the day, Judge Bailey announced that the jury was unable to reach a verdict and declared it a hung jury.

The final tally was eight for acquittal, four for conviction. The wives of the jurors were to blame for the outcome. While the jury was sequestered over the weekend, the bailiff allowed five of the jurors to see their wives. This angered some of the other jurors and the group came close to blows. This bitterness boiled over into the deliberation room, and after three separate votes, the jury called it quits.

At the announcement of a hung jury, Dr. Alexander sat up tall in his chair with a big smile. The doctor was then escorted by six police officers through a crowded mob and out of the courthouse. The doctor was free, for now. The prosecution would have eighteen months to decide if they would retry him again.

TRIAL OF RUFUS CANTRELL

During the trial of Dr. Alexander, the defense had actually laid the groundwork for Cantrell's defense. His attorney, Cass Conway, after unsuccessfully trying to get the charges dismissed, entered a plea of insanity. Cantrell's trial started on Monday, April 20, 1903, which was consumed with jury selection. Conway made a motion that made everyone in the courtroom gasp. He asked the court that at least half of the jury members be people of color from Marion County. Once the judge recovered from his shock, it was flatly denied. Cantrell would be tried by an all-white jury, mostly farmers who had already had an opinion about him before the case began.

Cass Connaway, defense attorney for Rufus Cantrell. *From the* Indianapolis News *February 6, 1903.*

The prosecution was prepared for an insanity defense. It took only two days to present the state's case with a dozen witnesses called. Prosecutor Ruckelshaus was prepared to submit evidence that Cantrell had fooled the War Department in securing his release from the army. Witnesses stated that Cantrell would eat

Rufus Cantrell's mug shot, Indiana State Prison. *Indiana State Archives.*

soap to produce foaming at the mouth in an attempt to get out of the army because the work was too hard.

The defense called Cantrell's mother to explain their family history. Cantrell's father, Bateman Cantrell, died in an insane asylum. His aunt Harriet was sent to an asylum for being "crazy." When Cantrell was young, he was thrown off a horse and landed on his head. From that time, he was prone to spasms. At the age of ten, he had a delusion that he was called by God to preach and believed that he could talk to God face to face. He was routinely exposed to taunting as a child in Tennessee. He had a violent temper and would become profane with anyone who challenged him. In Indianapolis, he suffered a heatstroke that left him incapacitated.

It only took four days to convict Cantrell of grave robbing. The all-white jury sentenced Cantrell to two to fourteen years in the state penitentiary. The jury rejected the insanity defense. There was outrage that Cantrell was found guilty while Dr. Alexander went free. Public consensus was that Dr. Alexander was guiltier than anyone, and regardless of race, everyone involved should be tried and convicted.

Prosecutor Ruckelshaus announced that there would be no new trial of Dr. Alexander. All of the ghouls who testified in the first trial refused to testify again. Even the thought of the doctor going free while they served time in prison undeterred them. With no witnesses to testify, Dr. Alexander escaped punishment, but public opinion was already against him.

TRIAL OF HAMPTON WEST

With Alexander's and Cantrell's cases concluded, attention was now focused on Noblesville. The grand jury returned an indictment against Hampton West and Lucius Stout for not only grave robbing but the murder of William Gray as well. West was still in jail while a warrant was issued for Stout.

Stout maintained his innocence and denied knowing Cantrell or West. He believed that the indictment was made against him to weaken his civil case against Tyler Cruthers and Horace W. Carey, the clerk of the circuit court in Hamilton County. His lawsuit claimed that Cruthers and Carey convinced him to go to Springfield, Illinois, to bet on a footrace in April 1902. Although Cruthers was the favorite to win the race, it was decided that Stout would bet on the local favorite, "Harry." Cruthers would intentionally fall, and Stout would win big betting on Harry. Instead, Harry went down and Cruthers crossed the finish line. Stout lost $3,100. He claimed that Cruthers and Carey were engaged in a con game, commonly known as bunco steering. Most residents felt that Stout got exactly what he deserved.

Whether by accident or by design, a couple of reporters from the *Indianapolis Sentinel* almost got West to confess. They went to the Noblesville jail to interview him. During the interview, they made some false statements, such as Cantrell and Stout both confessed to the crime and implicated him in the murder. After hearing that from the reporters, West asked for his attorney so that he could confess. West didn't have an attorney, so he asked for Stout's attorney, J. Frank Beals. Although West was not his client, Beals reassured West that no such statements were made by Stout and that he should refrain from talking to anyone, especially reporters.

It would take almost six months before West went to trial in July. Unable to make bond, he had been in the jail since early January. There would be no trial for his co-conspirator, Stout, as he escaped on a major technicality. There was a two-year statute of limitations based on the date of the indictment. Since Walter Manship's grave was robbed in January 1901 and Stout was indicted in March 1903, the charges against him were dropped. However, West was charged in December, a month before the limitations would have run out.

In anticipation of the trial, the residents of Fishers were planning a pretrial party. A number of residents had assembled scaffolding on Main Street for the purpose of burning those who were responsible for the grave robbing in effigy. Three dummies outfitted with old clothing and stuffed with inflammable material were hung by a noose. Above each dummy was a board with the words, "Bailey, Alexander, West." Citizens were still upset that Alexander escaped punishment and held Judge Bailey responsible since he presided over the trial.

As each dummy was hoisted up by the noose, the residents shouted, "Death to the graverobbers." After all three effigies were strung up, the residents proclaimed that they knew how to hand out justice if the courts could not. One of the spectators was going to set the dummies on fire, but the railroad agent protested that it could burn down the station. Instead, the dummies were cut down and burned together in the middle of the street while the residents rejoiced.

The courtroom was packed on the first day of the trial. When West was brought in, he was pale and sickly from his long confinement in the county jail. The prosecution was led by W.R. Fertig while West was represented by Newton Harding and Ralph Kane. The murder charge had been dropped, so West went on trial for theft—stealing Newton Bracken's body in September 1901.

The prosecution's case would rest heavily on the testimony of two ghouls, Cantrell and Sam Martin. They were both serving sentences in the Indiana Reformatory in Jeffersonville and were under guard while they were in Noblesville waiting to testify. The prosecution would take a week to present its case, ending with its last witness, Ralph Flanders. He testified that by accident, he ran into West near a thicket on his farm. He noticed that West was boiling a heavyset man in a large kettle. The body was missing a head. When Flanders asked West where he got the body, he said it was given to him by Dr. Alexander. The courtroom spectators could only shake their heads.

The defense's case was that West never knew Cantrell or Dr. Alexander and that he had an alibi for the night of the theft of Bracken's body. The lawyers called Stout as their first witness, and then most of West's family members testified that he was at home. Unbeknownst to the defense attorneys, West had written a letter to Rufus Cantrell when he was first jailed in January. He asked Cantrell to not testify against him. That letter would come back to haunt West, as it clearly showed a relationship between the two men.

The letter written to Cantrell on January 9, 1903:

Mr. Cantrell: I am in the Noblesville jail charged with robbing graves. I am an old man, fifty-seven years, nearly broken down. Mr. Cantrell, you know what you told me that you would not convict me, and I want to know what you are going to do. You have placed me in the position I am now in, and I am wanting to know what you will do.

I never wanted to talk to a man as bad as I do you. I want to see you and have a talk with you, but my lawyers advise me not to. I am sorry that I got so mad at you, as I did, but when we meet again I am in hopes it will be different. You have done me more injury than any man you ever implicated and you will think so when you think this over. Mr. Cantrell, you think this thing over to the best advantage to you and myself.

The reason I write you this letter, I saw an article in the paper about Joe Alexander and now I want you to consider this case of mine as I would consider your case if I were in your place. I see by the paper that you want to prepare to meet your God. Now, Mr. Cantrell, how can you do this if you convict me? Please answer by return mail.

Cantrell later responded to this letter that he would tell the truth when the time came.

From Indianapolis to Noblesville, every trial had surprises. During closing arguments, Prosecutor Fertig delivered a great speech to the jury—for a time, it was considered one of the most effective speeches ever given to a criminal jury in Indiana. But there was a reason for the passion behind the

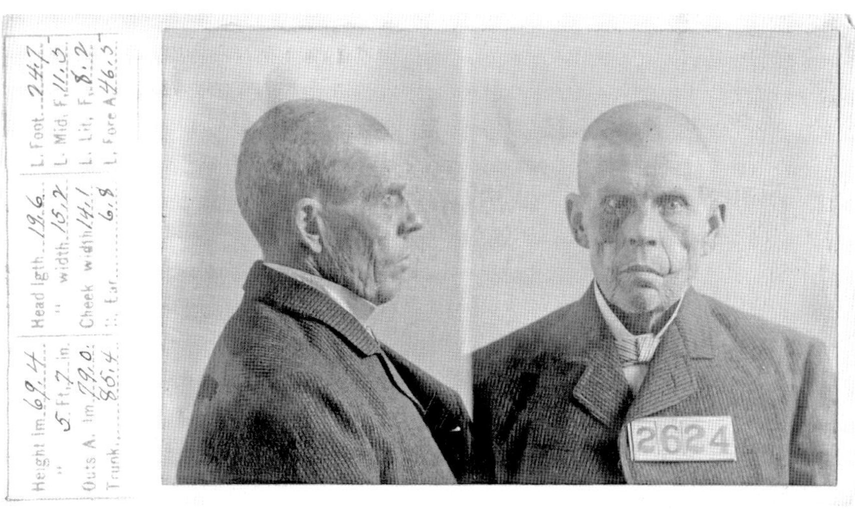

Wade Hampton West's mug shot, Indiana State Prison 1903. *Indiana State Archives.*

argument. Just prior to the trial, a member of the grand jury relayed to Fertig that Cantrell had confessed that he robbed the body of Jonah Fertig with the assistance of West. Jonah Fertig was Prosecutor Fertig's father, and this theft had occurred about five years before in the Williams Creek cemetery in Marion County. When the theft was discovered, authorities began to search the medical schools. A deal was struck that in exchange for $300, the body of Jonah Fertig would be turned over to them, as long as no questions were asked. The delivery and exchange of money took place near Carmel. The body was buried again the next day.

The jury found Hampton West guilty. The two things that ultimately led to his guilty verdict were Fertig's speech and the letter written to Cantrell. Before Judge Neal handed down West's sentence, he had some strong words for the state's chief witness, Cantrell. The judge considered Cantrell as one of the most "monumental liars of the century, a man who was utterly void of principle, self-respect and every other element that goes to make up a good citizen." West was sentenced to three to seven years in the state penitentiary in Michigan City.

VELMER FISHER

An urban legend was born out of the grave robbing trials. Velmer Fisher was the granddaughter of the city's founder, Salathiel Fisher, and she died at the age of three. She was buried in Beaver Cemetery (Highland Cemetery) in Fishers. Her father, Watson Fisher, did not want anyone disturbing her grave. Legend has it that her father lined her grave with nitroglycerin to ward off any would-be grave robbers. One shovel strike on the coffin would blow everyone up. There is much debate if the story is true, but there is only one way to find out and that legend will remain buried six feet under the ground.

Grave of three-year-old Velmer Fisher; located in Highland Cemetery (formerly Beaver Cemetery); legend has it that her father lined the grave with dynamite to ward off grave robbers. *Author's collection.*

Cold Case of Carrie Selvage

On the cold morning of March 11, 1900, Carrie Selvage walked away from the Union State Hospital in Indianapolis and was never seen again. Salvage was a former schoolteacher for the Indianapolis Public Schools. She suffered a nervous breakdown, and her family had her committed to the hospital.

The building, located at 1333 North Capitol Avenue, was originally the Indianapolis Orphans Asylum before it was converted into a hospital. At the time of her disappearance, she was wearing a dark blue nightgown with black felt slippers. She weighed only one hundred pounds, and because of an operation, her eyes were defective and shaped peculiarly.

The Indianapolis Police Department began a full-scale search. The hospital, surrounding areas and local businesses were searched. Bulletins and flyers were sent all across the country, and the search lasted for months. The department eventually drained the canal from Broad Ripple to its mouth, examining every crevice and hole in the hopes of locating the body. The family spent large amounts of money in the hopes of finding her. The body never turned up, and it was officially listed as a cold case.

While Cantrell was in Noblesville testifying at the West trial, he confessed to the detectives that he had knowledge of the disappearance of Carrie Selvage and knew where the body could be found. The case was still on the minds of many officers and detectives, and it was a case that many wanted to solve.

Cantrell explained to the detectives that after Selvage wandered away from the hospital, she was found by a ghoul from Hamilton County. He recognized her by the description that was posted around town. The ghoul took her to a farm in Hamilton County for about three weeks. She was then murdered using chloroform. They discussed selling her body, but because of the intense publicity surrounding her disappearance, she was instead buried about sixteen miles north of Noblesville.

Cantrell asked for clemency in exchange for taking the detectives to the burial spot. The detectives took Cantrell to the cemetery, and the body was exhumed. The body that was taken out of the ground was not Carrie Selvage. The detectives had been spending most of their time following up on this new information, and they felt that Cantrell was possibly making it up to get out of jail. Many, including the new superintendent of Jeffersonville Reformatory, were beginning to doubt some of Cantrell's confessions. He believed that Cantrell was seeking notoriety and barred Cantrell from making any more statements to the public.

Cantrell got everyone's hopes up, and they were still no closer to solving the case than they were in 1900.

Aftermath

To prevent and eliminate the business of grave robbing, the Indiana legislature passed House Bill 100 in 1903 just at the start of Dr. Alexander's trial. The act created a new State Anatomical Board headed by the president of the State Board of Health. The law provided how dead bodies were to be distributed to medical colleges and also laid out the penalties for violation of the law. The board was tasked with ensuring proper records were kept, receipts given and bodies were fairly distributed to the various colleges around the state.

The casualties of grave robbing were that some cemeteries actually "died." Greenlawn Cemetery was the first burial ground in Indianapolis, near Kentucky Avenue and Oliver Street. It was a prime location for grave robbers due to its proximity to downtown Indianapolis. It was believed that almost every grave had been robbed. Because of the cemetery's location along the White River, it was prone to flooding. As the city grew in population, a more modern cemetery was needed. The city decided to demolish the cemetery and reinter the bodies into the newer Crown Hill Cemetery. Surprisingly, there were not that many bodies to move.

After serving just one year in the Indiana State Penitentiary, Hampton West died from stomach cancer. His body was taken back to Fishers, where there was a small memorial service before he was buried in Crown Hill cemetery in Indianapolis. Fearing that his body would end up on the dissecting table like so many of his victims, West eventually confessed to the prison doctor that he had been a ghoul for nearly twenty years and stolen hundreds of bodies.

Although West was known for many things, he was also remembered for his courage and bravery. He was present for most of the major battles of the Civil War, and his face was partially disfigured from shrapnel. Cantrell, who was responsible for putting him jail, said, "West was the only man who ever ran me away from a grave."

Joseph C. Alexander was basically not welcome back in Fishers. When he did return to Fishers shortly after his trial to visit family, he and his wife were subjected to a major egging incident. Residents were hiding behind buildings waiting for the right moment to strike. The next morning, eggs were still everywhere in downtown—another reminder that they had not forgiven the favorite son. The doctor died in 1925 after having served as the plant physician for the Citizens Gas Company for most of the years after his trial.

Rufus Cantrell, "King of the Ghouls," served six years of his sentence before he was paroled in 1909. A stipulation of his parole was that he was to never maintain residence in the city of Indianapolis and he had to maintain permanent employment in some other part of the state. He moved to Anderson, Indiana, and got a job at the American Steel and Wire Company. He married Hattie Patterson, an eighteen-year-old girl, which ended in divorce five years later.

Cantrell's penchant for publicity was just as great when he got out of jail as it was before he went. He took his crime of grave robbing and turned it into a stage play. A local vaudeville theater in Anderson advertised that Cantrell along with three other ghouls would give a dramatized performance of their grave robbing exploits. There was so much anticipation for the play that people paid advance admission.

Shortly after his divorce in 1915, Cantrell moved to Michigan and began preaching again. He got remarried to May McConnell, a divorcée, but shortly after the wedding, authorities took both of them before the U.S. Commissioner of Immigration. The wedding took place in Windsor, Canada, as McConnell claimed to be Canadian, but she was in fact a U.S. citizen. The immigration department considered deporting her for being an undesirable citizen.

Rufus and his new wife were made for each other. She was a major in the Charity Army of America, known for scamming people out of their money in the name of charity. The organization was eventually shut down. Cantrell began preaching in Detroit at the Gospel Praise Mission, but he was anything but a man of God. He was charged along with his aide, Eldridge Gowdy, for theft from his parishioners. Every time Cantrell made a house call, he would leave with money and valuables. While Cantrell preached sermons, Gowdy would pick the pockets of men and women while they were on their knees praying. They were both sentenced to the Marquette Penitentiary for two years. Coincidentally, his wife's first husband was also serving time there. Cantrell was paroled on September 10, 1918, and what became of him after that is a mystery.

The grave robbing investigation did much to advance the careers of Detectives Asch and Manning. A few years after the trials, Asch was promoted to captain of the detective bureau. Then in 1909, he was involved in an international incident while on vacation. He went back to his birthplace in Strasbourg, and while he was there, he was arrested by the German police for having evaded military service at the time that he came to the United States. As a captain with the Indianapolis Police Department, he was also

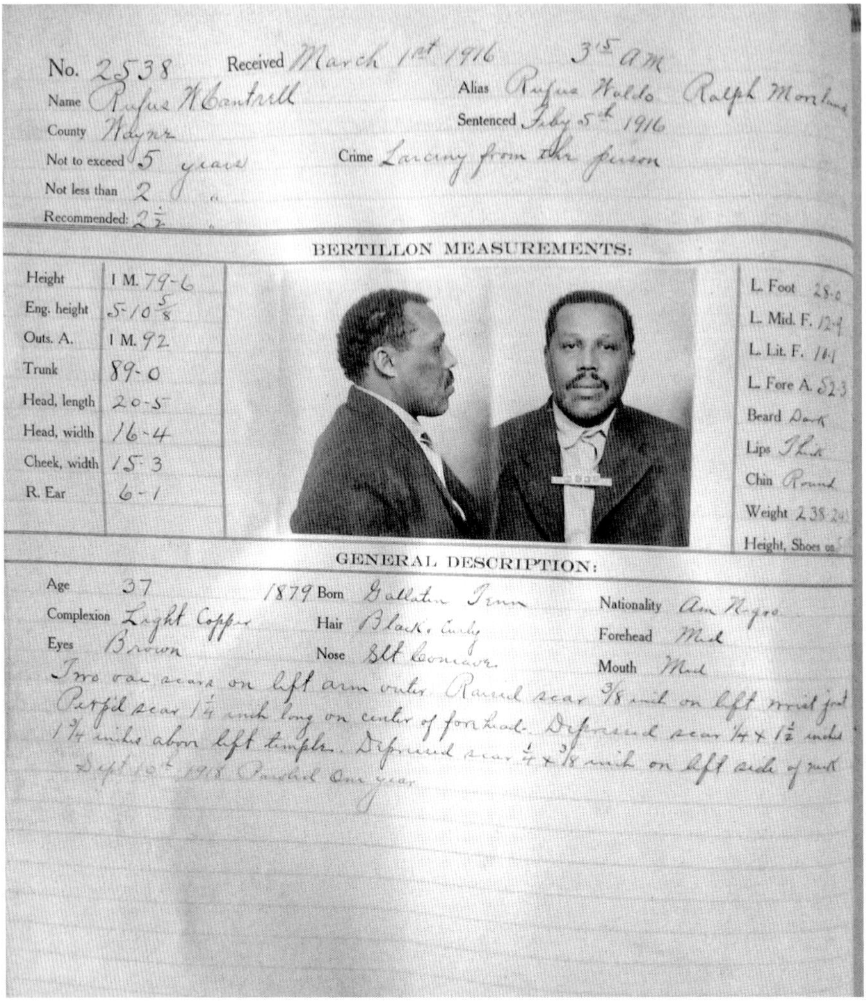
No. 2538 Received March 1st 1916 3:15 am
Name Rufus H Cantrell Alias Rufus Waldo Ralph Morland
County Wayne Sentenced Feby 5th 1916
Not to exceed 5 years Crime Larceny from the person
Not less than 2 "
Recommended: 2½ "

BERTILLON MEASUREMENTS:

Height	1 M. 79-6
Eng. height	5-10 5/8
Outs. A.	1 M. 92
Trunk	89-0
Head, length	20-5
Head, width	16-4
Cheek, width	15-3
R. Ear	6-1

L. Foot	28-0
L. Mid. F.	12-4
L. Lit. F.	10-1
L. Fore A.	52-3
Beard	Dark
Lips	Thick
Chin	Round
Weight	238
Height, Shoes on	

GENERAL DESCRIPTION:

Age 37 1879 Born Gallatin Tenn Nationality Am Negro
Complexion Light Copper Hair Black, Curly Forehead Med
Eyes Brown Nose Slt Concave Mouth Med
Two vac scars on left arm outer. Raised scar 3/8 inch on left wrist front. Pitted scar 1/4 inch long on center of forehead. Depressed scar 1/4 x 1½ inches 1¾ inches above left temple. Depressed scar 1/4 x 3/8 inch on left side of neck.
Sept 10th 1918 Paroled One year

Rufus Cantrell's mug shot, Marquette Prison, Michigan. *Archives of Michigan; Michigan History Center.*

being subjected to a court-martial. The U.S. consulate intervened on his behalf, and he was granted a pardon and allowed to return to his position with the police force. Detective Asch died in 1914 at the age of fifty-seven.

Detective Chauncey Manning held every position in the detective bureau before he retired from the Indianapolis Police Department in 1928. After retirement, he worked for the newly created State Bureau of Criminal Investigation & Identification (now the Indiana State Police.) He died a few years later, in 1932, of heart disease.

Before Manning died, he was able to get closure on the one case that stumped him his entire career, the missing person case of Carrie Selvage. By 1920, the Union State Hospital had closed down. In the subsequent years, it operated as a boardinghouse and as a garage. In April 1920, workers were installing a steel beam in the roof of the building when they came across something unusual. In the attic was a skeleton leaning against the wall with the skull on the ground. The skeleton was wearing a dark blue nightgown and black slippers.

The body was positively identified as Carrie Selvage. She was in a second attic that was unknown to most people. Obviously she never escaped the hospital, nor was she murdered and buried as Cantrell had claimed. Instead, the consensus was that she went to the attic and possibly either starved herself or froze to death.

The cold case of Carrie Selvage was officially closed.

11

THE GREAT SCHOOL CONTROVERSY

It appears that our township officials, who are being directed by a few master minds, are not going to be satisfied until Delaware Township is bankrupt and doomed to oblivion.
—a disillusioned taxpayer

Residents of Hamilton County have always been passionate about their children's education. In the early days, a teacher was not guaranteed a job year after year. At annual school meetings, residents of the community would vote on whether to keep or fire the current teachers. These meetings would usually become heated, and on more than one occasion, they ended in physical altercations.

In the 1950s, a school controversy arose within the three southern townships of the county: Clay, Delaware and Fall Creek. This controversy would lead to the creation of two new political parties. It would also lead to the passing of a legislative bill that would forever change the geographic boundaries of two of those townships. Although most of the squabbling took place during the 1950s, it actually began a lot earlier than that.

In April 1823, the Indiana legislature created Hamilton County. The first act was to elect county commissioners, county officials and judges. William Dyer, Zenis Beckwith and Solomon Finch were the first elected county commissioners. The first order of business was to divide the county into two townships, White River in the north and Delaware in the south. This meeting took place at the home of William Connor, one of the original settlers of Delaware Township. Because of Connor, Delaware Township would have the first brick house and trading post in Hamilton County.

Townships are local units of government and political subdivisions of a county. Townships are governed by an elected trustee, and primary responsibilities include road maintenance, trash collection and upkeep of cemeteries. But in the 1800s in Hamilton County, the townships had a lot more political and law enforcement power. The townships had elected constables that would enforce laws in the rural areas within their townships, and elected township judges would usually hold court, sometimes at their homes. An appeal of a township judge's sentence would automatically go to the Hamilton County Courthouse in Noblesville. But most importantly, the townships controlled the schools; in some ways, the township was more powerful than the county itself.

In 1833, Delaware and White River Township would be carved up to create seven new additional townships in Hamilton County. Jackson, Washington, Wayne and Adams would combine with White River in the north and Noblesville Township in the center of the county, while Delaware, Clay and Fall Creek occupied the south. Clay Township stretched from Boone County to Rangeline Road, Delaware Township went from Rangeline Road to present-day State Road 37 and Fall Creek picked up continuing all the way to Madison County.

The White River split Delaware Township almost down the middle. Residents commonly referred to their township as either East or West Delaware depending on what side of the river they were located. In 1875, a proposal was made to eliminate Delaware Township using the White River as a natural boundary to connect Clay with Fall Creek. Reasons for the elimination of the township were financial, as it reduced salaries for elected officials; political, as it decreased the number of voting precincts; and educational, as not all schools were created equal.

Schools in Delaware Township had advanced a great deal from the time that the first school was established in 1830, in a log cabin owned by Abraham Williams. One such school was Carmel Academy, later renamed Carmel High School, which was built in 1868 by the Quakers. At the time, the school was the best in the county. It was a two-story brick building and was the first to have the brand-new Allen and Grant desks, which were patented in 1869 in Richmond, Indiana. Carmel Academy started off as a private school, but due to financial reasons, it became a public school and was leased to Delaware Township. Students from outside Delaware Township could attend for $10 a month ($190 in 2020 dollars). Delaware

Township had the only two high schools (K–12), Carmel and Fishers, while Clay and Fall Creek only had one elementary school. Delaware Township seemed to have the best educational opportunities in the county, and this began to create jealousy between Clay and Fall Creek Townships.

In June 1875, the board of county commissioners formally dismissed the idea of eliminating Delaware Township. An argument was made that using the White River as a dividing line for the township boundary would make an awkward and disproportionate line. The north line of Clay Township would be almost thirteen miles long while the south boundary line would be eight to ten miles long and only five miles wide. That was a big change from the perfect square that encompassed the township. Another issue was that the White River encircles a body of land as it flows toward Indianapolis. This island of ten acres would certainly lead to disagreements between Clay and Fall Creek if Delaware were to be eliminated.

The matter was put to rest until 1912, when a large group of farmers began circulating two petitions that proposed, once again, that Delaware Township be eliminated. Finally, in August 1913, the county commissioners voted to hold an election on the twenty-sixth of that month in the three townships to decide on whether to consolidate the three townships into two.

The reasons for the consolidation were pretty much unchanged from 1875. Residents on the east side of the river were against a tax increase to build a library and a new school building in Carmel. Economy and convenience were the driving forces behind the consolidation. However, residents in Fall Creek were not as supportive for consolidation as Delaware and Clay. Since Fall Creek had no secondary school, its students were sent to Fishers. Fall Creek Township had to pay Delaware thirty-two dollars for each student to be educated. It was costing Delaware Township fifty dollars to educate their students. So therefore, if the consolidation happened, they would have to pay more, but as it stands, they were saving a lot of money. A bill had been introduced in the Indiana legislature to eliminate this loophole, and it would make Fall Creek have to pay its fair share for education.

The township consolidation plan was met with defeat. The decades went by, and in 1945, a new plan was hatched. A petition had circulated among the residents advocating for one high school to serve all three townships, and it was to be built in the geographic center of the three townships. The new school system would be called the Southern Consolidated Schools of Hamilton County. This plan failed. Then in 1945, Forest Groff, county superintendent of schools, proposed making a metropolitan school district for just Clay and Delaware Townships. This would have been accomplished

Fall Creek Township school bus driven by Charles Randall. *Larry A. Reynolds.*

by building one new high school for the two townships and then using the existing high school buildings at Fishers and Carmel for grade schools. This plan also failed to gain support.

To better manage the Carmel school, which was jointly funded by Clay and Delaware Townships, a school board was formed. The Carmel School Board was the only one of its kind in Hamilton County. The board consisted of Superintendent Forrest Groff, Omer Beaver and Doyle Ramsey, Delaware and Clay Township trustees, respectively. The newly formed school board was hailed as a huge progressive step in the history of the county.

In the summer of 1951, township consolidation was once again discussed in the southern part of the county. In order for the consolidation to proceed, petitions containing 51 percent of freeholders in each township had to be secured before the county commissioners could act on the proposal. After almost seventy-five years and numerous defeats at the polls, victory seemed to have finally been achieved. The county auditor, Harry Griffin, confirmed that the required signatures had been acquired and the proponents of consolidation could celebrate.

That victory would soon be replaced with yet another defeat in a cruel and most unusual way. Just two days after victory had been declared, forty-six freeholders from Fall Creek filed a motion to withdraw their names from the petition. That meant that Fall Creek was below the 51 percent threshold and the township consolidation was thrown into disarray. Proponents of the consolidation described the move as an atomic bomb detonating. Even the county attorney, Frank S. Campbell, was perplexed—there wasn't any precedent to follow. This was the first of its kind, and it would take a judge to sort out the mess.

The reasons for the withdrawal were that the township revision had changed since the original petition had been circulated, and some felt that the division of the township was no longer necessary. But many felt that the real reason was because of $80,000 that was in a building fund that Fall Creek did not want to share. That building fund was to be allocated to build a new grade school since Bethlehem Elementary, Fall Creek's only school, was closed down in 1951 because of its poor condition. That left them with no school, and the only other elementary school was in a rural part of Clay Township known as Clay Center. Since they had money set aside to build a new school, the "objectors" felt that the school crisis didn't concern them.

The county commissioners were faced with a dilemma. They had to decide whether to accept the three petitions as they were or discard them. The commissioners eventually sided with the proponents of consolidation and ordered the division to take place. The opponents immediately appealed the decision to the circuit court of Hamilton County.

A special judge, Sam Offutt of Greenfield, was brought in to hear the case. Judge Offutt found for the Fall Creek objectors and allowed them to remove their names from the petition and thereby halted the division of Delaware Township. As soon as the decision was handed down, it was appealed again to the Indiana Court of Appeals. In November 1953, the appeals court dismissed the case without a hearing, upholding Judge Offutt's ruling. A victory that seemed to have been almost certain took two and a half years to arbitrate, only to end in another defeat.

For all that Fall Creek did to contribute to the defeat of the township consolidation plan, there was an ironic turn of events. In July 1953, just six months after the appeals court handed down its decision, Fall Creek began trying to start the consolidation plan again. Fall Creek Township's trustee, Clarence Russell, was concerned about rising tuition charges. Since Fall Creek did not have a high school of its own, its students must rely on Fishers, Noblesville or Fortville. Schools had been recently granted the authority to raise tuition by as much as $100 to pay for school construction costs. Fall Creek had 150 students at Fishers; 95 students at Fortville; and 7 students at Noblesville, totaling just under $40,000 per school year that it had to pay the other townships. Now that Fall Creek had a school crisis of its own, the residents were ready to play ball with Clay and Delaware.

As the petitions for township consolidation began circulating, a new political party was being formed in Delaware Township. The Better Schools Party advocated for school consolidation between Clay and Delaware Townships and was opposed to eliminating Delaware as a township. Represented by a school bell superimposed on a book, the new party listed Charles Ober as candidate for trustee and Russell Henry, William Newby and Joseph Payne as candidates for the advisory board. They would compete with the Republicans, who supported the township division plan, while the Democrats were hoping to cash in on the squabble between the two.

In Fall Creek Township, another political party formed. The Citizens Party supported the township division plan while both the Republican and Democrats opposed it. This new party was formed because Delaware Township raised the tuition charges of Fall Creek students, which led to bitterness between the two townships. Charles Whelchel, a bus driver in Fall Creek for twenty years, was nominated for trustee.

More bitterness erupted in Delaware Township when the three-man advisory board refused to sign the budget because eleven students who should have attended Fishers were instead enrolled in Carmel, which was jointly funded by Delaware and Clay Townships. The parents of these eleven students were members of the Better Schools Party. They argued that the school in Fishers was below standard and they had every right to send their children to whatever school they desired.

Fishers High School was built in 1908. But over the next forty years, the school had not kept up with advancements in education. The school offered a basic curriculum and lacked important courses like physics. School facilities were lacking; there was only one sink in the chemistry lab. Trade courses such as agriculture and mechanics were nonexistent. From a health standpoint, there was only one bathroom for 175 girls. The Better Schools Party made a valid argument for sending their kids to Carmel. Although Delaware Township would have to pay more tuition for these eleven students, Sam Pursell, township trustee, disagreed with his own board and expressed no objection to the students enrolling at Carmel.

Clay Township was the only one that wasn't experiencing political turmoil. There was no opposition to the Republican candidate for trustee, Dan Stuckey. However, he was still concerned with the problems in Delaware Township since Carmel High School was jointly funded between the two.

As the election neared, tensions rose, especially in Delaware Township. The Better Schools Party had started to publish its own newsletter, the *Delaware Vigilante*. The opposing parties began plastering flyers around town proclaiming "The Vigilantes are Coming." Even the local newspaper, the *Noblesville Ledger*, began referring to the members as Vigilantes.

The political campaign was already being referred to as "The Battle at White River." There had never been an issue that aroused the voters of these three townships more than what do about their schools. This was one of the bitterest campaigns since the county was torn apart by Theodore Roosevelt's Bull Moose Party.

While Fall Creek would be voting on township division, Delaware and Clay Townships would be voting on whether to consolidate their schools. If consolidation passed, a seven-member school board would be established with all the schools under their control. If it failed, the current system would remain.

Election Day saw one of the best voter turnouts in the county. Delaware and Fall Creek had over 75 percent turnout, while Clay, without much to vote on, had 67 percent. It was not a good day for the Better Schools Party, as the school consolidation plan was defeated. Only one in six precincts favored the plan. As expected, Dan Stuckey was elected Clay Township trustee. Republican Van Eller was elected trustee of Delaware Township along with two of his running mates for the advisory board. The only Better School Party victory went to Dr. Russell Henry, who won by three votes. Republican Paul Wood won trustee in Fall Creek.

Now that school consolidation was defeated at the polls, that opened up the door for township division. Fall Creek, which had sabotaged efforts previously, stated that it had enough signatures to push it through. While all other plans had been met with defeat, the one plan that had a majority support was to combine West Delaware with Clay Township and East Delaware would be left to form its own small township.

This required legislative approval. With the assistance of State Representative Robert S. Webb and State Senator Glen Neaville, the bill to divide up Delaware Township passed by a vote of 53–33. Indiana law dictates that a township has to be at least twenty-four square miles. By splitting up Delaware Township at the river, the new township east of the river would be only fifteen square miles. Senator Neaville led the effort to change it from twenty-four square miles to twelve. This law change paved the way for the division, and it would also affect nine other townships within the state.

With the township division imminent, Van Eller announced that an addition would be added to Fishers High School. The addition would include two new classrooms, a cafeteria, a kitchen and more restrooms. Fishers High School was the smallest in the county serving grades K–12. The school became a focal point during the campaign, with some residents

Fishers High School in 1959, with the new grade school addition. *Larry A. Reynolds.*

advocating for its elimination. The new addition would relieve overcrowding and offer an expanded curriculum, all things that had been addressed by the Better Schools Party.

The division of Delaware Township became official on August 1, 1955. Many residents in the "new" and greatly reduced Delaware Township were not thrilled with the division. The township division left Delaware with a low amount of taxable property because more than half went to Clay Township. Delaware had the highest tax rate in the county but because there wasn't enough taxable property, there wasn't sufficient revenue to operate twelve grades of school. Ironically, once again, it was Delaware Township wanting to consolidate with Fall Creek. But with a lower tax rate, no debt and a brand-new elementary school, Fall Creek had no desire.

Eighty years after the first proposal was made and numerous defeats, it took legislative action to solve the school problems plaguing the southern townships. Delaware Township, the oldest and once the largest township, is now the smallest township in the county. School corporations have since replaced township-controlled schools. Carmel-Clay controls all schools within Clay Township, while Hamilton Southeastern controls all schools within Delaware and Fall Creek Townships. Part of the Fishers High School was torn down in 1967, but the addition that was added in 1955 remains and is now Fishers Elementary School.

12

THE MYSTERIOUS TRITTIPO BOMBINGS

How his muscle has hardened since he was taken to manual labor. Why, when he quit business a few months ago he only weighed 115 pounds, and now he tips the beam at 115 and half pounds.

—statement made in jest as Sam Trittipo built his new building in Fishers

History books credit Salathiel Fisher with founding the town that bears his name. In 1872, he platted the first sections along the railroad tracks. However, there was a sizeable percentage of the population that, although they agreed with that statement, perhaps wished it could be different. In their minds, Fishers was actually founded in 1886 when Samuel Trittipo moved his mercantile store from New Britton to the growing town of Fishers Station. But who was the man so many people considered the "true" founder of Fishers?

Samuel Trittipo came to Indiana in 1838 when he was eight years old. His parents moved from Virginia, and they originally settled in Germantown. Upon turning eighteen, he left for California to strike it rich along with all of the other gold rushers. After a year and a half, he returned to Indiana and settled in New Britton. He opened up a mercantile store that he would operate for nearly fifty years until his death. Although he was known for being a well-respected and successful businessman, he was also the town's postmaster for nearly twenty years.

There was perhaps no person more beloved and revered than Sam Trittipo or "T," as he was commonly referred. Trittipo believed in a strong community and that everyone should strive to be a good neighbor. He might have been a businessman, but he also recognized the importance of giving back to the community. He gave free use of the upstairs of his business to church groups and other organizations that needed a place to meet but couldn't afford to pay rent.

On Trittipo's fifty-second birthday, over one hundred people of New Britton surprised him with a lavish party that was fit for a king. His home had been turned into a banquet hall. Tables were filled with food, drinks and desserts. Trittipo and his wife were seated at the head of the table. A string band from Germantown provided the live entertainment. The people of New Britton went out of their way to show their love and respect for one of the most important people in the town, and it was a true testament to the respect that he garnered.

In 1886, Trittipo made a hard decision to move his business a couple of miles up the street to the rapidly growing town of Fishers Station. After securing a prime location near the railroad tracks on Main Street, Trittipo started building the foundation for his new store. A two-story brick building with a glass front with ironworks reclaimed from a railroad station on Tenth Street in Indianapolis would totally transform this small town.

When Sam Trittipo left New Britton, the clock had started as to how long the town would continue to survive. The residents of Fishers Station welcomed him with open arms while New Britton mourned his departure. While he viewed the move to Fishers Station as strictly a business decision, it never changed who he was as a person.

Less than a year after moving to Fishers Station, business was booming. Sam Trittipo enlisted his son, Albert, to enter the family business, and they were partners for over a decade until a family feud.

As much as Sam Trittipo was revered and respected, there were some who had different opinions. They were strong enough that death was the only alternative.

In the early morning hours of Saturday, January 24, 1892, an explosion ripped through the Trittipo farm and almost took Albert's life. It was just another typical morning as Albert went to the barn to do his usual chores. When he opened the stable door, he was greeted with a bright flash and then his ears were rocked by a loud explosion caused by a homemade pipe bomb.

The bomb, a two-inch pipe, eighteen inches long, was filled with buckshot and nitroglycerine. The bomb was attached to the door with springs, and the moment that the door was swung open, the bomb detonated. Thanks to Mother Nature, his life was spared. Because of the heavy snowfall, a

Sam Trittipo's store as seen around the turn of the twentieth century. *Jim Beehler.*

snowbank had formed in front of the barn door. The door did not swing open as easily it should have. This is most certainly what saved his life. Had the door opened like it should, he would have been directly in front of the bomb, but as it was, he escaped with his life. His face was still badly burned.

The bomb was successful in blowing out the bottom of the door large enough that a calf could enter. The bomb embedded over five hundred pellets into the wood of the barn and destroyed the Trittipos' buggy. A horse that was in the stable at the time of the explosion was unharmed but was so badly frightened it refused to go back into the stable the next day.

The town was shocked at the news of the attempted murder of Albert Trittipo. There was suspicion about who might have built the "infernal machine." A few days later, he received a note from one of the people responsible for the bomb.

The note read: "Death will come by powder and led to both of you. Now git. Traps now fixt to your buildings redey to tuch off. Now go." The note contained many spelling errors, and whether it was done intentionally or not was still under investigation.

Whether the bomb was meant for Sam or Albert is not entirely clear. But about a month later, Samuel Trittipo had a chance encounter with some "unknown" persons who might have been responsible for the bomb. As he went to the barn very early on a Sunday morning, he was approached by two men. Sam was subjected to a barrage of name calling and derogatory statements. Sensing that this might become a dangerous situation, he went back to his house and retrieved his revolver.

Sam Trittipo might have had a heart of gold, but at the age of sixty-two, he showed that his generosity should not be taken for granted and that he would do what was necessary to protect his family. He could have stayed in the house until the people left, but Sam returned with his revolver. Sam was subjected to another series of personal attacks, which rose to threats of violence. Sam was not about to back down. He presented his revolver at the men and told them to do their worst. The shiny revolver made the men think twice, and they left the area. Sam made it known that he would not back down from a fight.

The culprits who set the bomb were never identified, and life went on in town as usual. In 1893, Albert Trittipo was appointed postmaster of Fishers Station. Sam Trittipo, who had been postmaster of New Britton for decades, resigned in 1886 when he moved to Fishers Station. He would resume his postmaster duties in his new town until Albert took over.

In 1895, another attempt was made on Albert Trittipo's life. This time, a lot more ingenuity went into the design and delivery of the bomb than it had in 1892. Since Albert was the postmaster, what better way to send a bomb than through the mail.

The box addressed to Albert Trittipo looked like any of the thousand boxes that went through the post office on a daily basis. The box was small, measuring six inches long, four inches wide and three inches deep. But inside the box was a carefully designed bomb capable of blowing up a large building.

Albert Trittipo standing inside the general store. *Jim Beehler.*

Inside the box was a stick of dynamite that had been wrapped tightly with twine, and the box was filled with over ten pounds of gunpowder, until the dynamite was completely submerged. Attached to the lid of the box was a row of matches with the heads lying on a piece of sandpaper also covered in gunpowder.

The package did not arouse any suspicion when Albert Trittipo picked it up. "These are samples" was written on the outside of the package, and he just assumed it was advertisement materials. Since he normally received these types of packages daily, he failed to notice the instructions on the box requiring him to open it from a particular end.

As he opened the box from the end opposite of the instructions, he immediately noticed the bomb. If he had opened it up from the other end, the matches attached to the lid would slide across the sandpaper, igniting the gunpowder, detonating the dynamite.

Albert Trittipo immediately informed the post office inspector, W.T. Fletcher. A further investigation of the incident revealed that the package was sent from Cincinnati. It was believed that the bomb was manufactured by someone in Fishers Station, and in an attempt to confuse investigators, the bomb was transported to Cincinnati and mailed back to Fishers Station. Just like with the bombing incident in 1892, no suspects were ever identified.

Why these bombings occurred or who was responsible has always been a mystery. The two bombing incidents involved Albert Trittipo, so like any criminal investigation, the theory of who committed the crime should start there. Although his father was well respected, Albert was rougher around the edges and didn't mind challenging authority. In 1889, the Fishers Town Council passed an ordinance that all persons living in Fishers Station were required to keep their streets and alleys clean. The town marshal was vested with the power to fine those who refused, no more than five dollars and no less than one.

A few months after the first bombing incident in 1892, Albert Trittipo refused to clean his street and alleys as required by ordinance. Fishers town marshal Dan Socks fined Albert $1.25, which he refused to pay. At the regular scheduled meeting of the town council, the board filed a civil suit against Albert. The town hired W.S. Christian, a well-respected lawyer in Noblesville, to represent it. The case was moved to Carmel and tried before Judge Small to eliminate any conflicts of interest. The judge ruled in favor of Fishers. It was appealed to the Hamilton County Circuit Court, who found in favor of the town, and Albert Trittipo was required to pay the fine. The fine, $1.25, was far less than what the town paid for attorney and witness fees, but it sent a message that all persons are required to obey the law.

The Trittipos were also active in the Prohibition movement. They warned citizens of the dangers of the evils of the saloon. In a town where whiskey flowed like a river, that could have very well led to a death sentence. The Trittipos were well respected, and they were heavily involved in the Democratic Party, in which they wielded enormous political power. Some of the locals may have been threatened by their political power if they used it to shut down the saloons.

W.S. Christian; prominent Noblesville attorney, hired by Fishers Town Council to prosecute Albert Trittipo. *From the* Enterprise, *November 13, 1908.*

Albert Trittipo was the plaintiff and defendant in numerous civil court cases during his career. The various people that he sued or were sued by could have easily been a suspect in the bombings. Even in a small town, bad blood exists between neighbors and sometimes within their own family.

When Sam Trittipo became business partners with his son, it was agreed that Albert would run the store while Sam supplied the capital. For the next decade, Sam invested a considerable amount of money into the business without taking hardly any of it out. Albert, on the other hand, withdrew over $5,000 (approximately $156,000 in 2020) during that time. In 1899, it was finally revealed when Sam, true to his good nature, agreed to sell the second story of his building to the local lodge, No. 440, of the Independent Order of Odd Fellows (IOOF), which was desperately looking for a place to hold meetings.

Albert refused to sign the deed over to the IOOF although Sam had already been paid for half interest in the property. Sam filed a civil suit asking that a receiver be appointed to sell off the merchandise and to force his son to sell the property. The case was decided in favor of Albert, and Sam's motion for a new trial was denied. The case finally made its way to the Indiana Supreme Court two years later. Once again, the high court found in favor of Albert, and the case was finally settled.

The bitterness between father and son was clearly evident to everyone. There was a sense of betrayal that Albert would take advantage of his father. There was sadness that Sam had to resort to suing his son, something that no father would wish for. In the end, Sam's generosity was overshadowed by his son's greed. Sam died a little more than a year later of lung problems with no indication that they ever reconciled.

Perhaps the attack on Albert Trittipo had nothing to do with his disdain for authority or his penchant for suing others, but it could have been a case of mistaken identity. There appears to have been another Albert Trittipo in Fishers Station who was involved in a lot of criminal activity. In 1893, about six months after Albert was appointed postmaster of Fishers Station, another Al Trittipo, along with a known criminal, Charles Leaming, stole a horse and buggy that belonged to a county commissioner. The horse and buggy were discarded in Bloomfield, Indiana, and the suspects were eventually caught and given jail sentences.

Later in 1898, that same Al Trittipo, along with two others, was arrested for assaulting a bartender at a saloon, characterized as an unprovoked attack. Trittipo was fined forty-five dollars for the attack and another ten for assaulting a patron at the same bar the night before. Unable to pay the fine, Trittipo was locked up in the county jail for six months. It is plausible that the attacks on Albert Trittipo, the postmaster, were meant for the younger Al Trittipo.

Sam Trittipo's building; the American Legion occupied it for a time. *Larry A. Reynolds.*

Looking more closely at the life of Albert Trittipo, the list of suspects seems to be endless. But the mystery becomes even more complicated. Albert's younger brother Vora, previously the agent of the Fishers railroad station, would eventually go into the family business. However, his business specialized in cigars and would be totally independent of his brother.

In July 1912, the town council approved Vora's request for a license to operate a pool hall. The license needed to be renewed yearly. He paid all of his fees and obeyed all of the laws. However, on March 21, 1914, Vora became the next target. In the early morning hours, around 2:00 a.m., a stick of dynamite was thrown through the basement window. The explosion blew a hole into the concrete floor, destroyed every pool table and blew out every window. The force of the explosion was said to have shook every building in town. Just like with the incidents with Albert Trittipo, the bombing of Vora's pool hall was never solved.

With the crimes unsolved, we are left with only theories and speculations about why the Trittipo family was the only one subjected to these violent attacks. The story may always remain a mystery.

13

TURKEY SHOOT LEADS TO MURDER

Now a man may shoot his fellow down and leisurely walk away and escape. Is human life less valuable now than ever before, or have people become so hardened in feeling and so selfish that they regard life taking as a sort of amusement to be indulged in at will by outlaws?…If something is not done, we will soon become a land of murderers.
—opinion by a Fishers resident regarding the murder of James Redwine, January 7, 1876

Christmas is normally a festive time, but in the winter of 1875, it turned tragic, and a turkey shoot became the setting for Fishers's first reported homicide.

Turkey shoots are a time-honored tradition dating all the way back to the Puritans. When wild turkeys were in abundance across the nation, the Puritans used turkey shoots to supply people with food. Over the years, turkey shoots became popular sporting events, mostly in rural communities.

As the wild turkey population declined, farmers sought an opportunity to capitalize by making a profit on domestic turkeys. Farmers could make money on their turkeys, while a good marksman could supply his family with enough food for the holidays and make a net gain from the cost of the turkey shoot.

The popularity of turkey shoots continued to grow. In 1936, Carmel hosted the largest turkey shoot in the United States up to that time; the event lasted three days, with over 1,000 people in attendance and 378 large turkeys up for prizes. But as with any competitive sport, tempers sometimes flare up, and this is exactly what happened on Christmas Eve 1875 in Fishers Station.

Residents came together that morning to participate in a turkey shoot held at Lowry Woods. The property owned by a local farmer, Enoch Lowry, was about a mile and half south of Fishers Station. Everything was calm until between 1:00 and 2:00 p.m., when a dispute arose between James Redwine and Milford "Dick" Parsley. The dispute began when Parsley claimed that he shot the target, thereby winning the turkey. Redwine countered that the shot was made earlier that morning. Within a few minutes, shots rang out, and Redwine was hit. He would die at ten o'clock on Christmas morning.

Six hours after Redwine's death, Coroner Edgar Loehr, Deputy Prosecutor Francis Householder and Charles Potter took the train from Noblesville to Fishers Station to investigate the incident. Edgar Loehr was one of the most well-respected physicians in the country and spent most of his life in Hamilton County. He went to the Indiana University at Bloomington for his undergraduate degree and then went to the Ohio Medical College at Cincinnati, graduating with a medical degree in 1871. Upon returning to Noblesville, he went into practice with Dr. J.M. Gray, who had an office above Truitt's drugstore on the Noblesville Square.

In 1875, Dr. Loehr was elected the county coroner. By the time of the shooting in Fishers Station, Dr. Loehr was well experienced. His first maiden trip as coroner was in March of that year when he was summoned to investigate the murder of a local billiards club owner, John Jamison, whose club was on the same square as his medical practice. After arriving at the house, he discovered that the man was not dead but in severe pain. During an accidental discharge, his wife had fired a revolver and the bullet had struck him in the groin, lodging deep inside his scrotum.

All three visitors from Noblesville were ambitious people but politically different. The murder investigation of James Redwine would help to boost their reputations in the county. Dr. Loehr was heavily involved in Republican politics. Besides a term as county coroner, Dr. Loehr would eventually become mayor of Noblesville from 1910 to 1917.

Francis Householder and Charles Potter were practicing attorneys, and both aspired to being elected as the prosecuting attorney for the Twenty-Fourth Judicial District, which covered both Hamilton and Madison Counties. Householder was a strong Democrat who served a term as prosecuting attorney in 1878 but was not reelected in 1880 when the Republicans were accused of substituting another person on the ballot in his place in order to secure a victory for the Republican challenger. As a consolation prize, he was appointed county school superintendent in 1881. He would also be appointed postmaster of Noblesville from 1885 to 1887.

Upon arriving in Fishers Station, they went to the home of James Redwine and, after a brief investigation, determined that an inquest was needed to determine exactly how his death came about. A list was composed of potential jurors, and the list included prominent men in the community.

The list of men summoned was like a who's who of Fishers Station: William Bolton, William Northam, James Flanagan, Charles Parton and Bartholomew Irwin. After the trial, many of these men would go on to become constables, justices of the peace and postmasters. George Seymour, the elected constable of Delaware Township, was instructed to find these men so the trial could commence.

During the inquest, four witnesses were interviewed. The accounts given by John Perkins, N. Johnson, Enoch Lowry and David Redwine, father of the deceased, all testified to the same version of events.

The turkey shoot had been going on for about six hours by the time Dick Parsley and James Redwine stepped to the line. With every intention of winning a Christmas turkey, they raised their rifles, took aim and fired at the target.

Parsley's brother, Taylor, claimed that his brother had the winning shot. Redwine disagreed and told Taylor that the shot he was referring to was made that morning.

Redwine pointed at his shot on the target and confidently exclaimed, "This was the shot that takes the turkey."

Milford Parsley had walked up and responded angrily, "You are a damned liar." Redwine returned the compliment.

As the argument began to get heated, Redwine took his rifle from his shoulder and handed it to his father. Redwine took a couple of steps back and said, "If that is your game, all right."

The dispute was going to be settled with fists until the last man was standing. They lunged at each other, each one striking the other numerous times. Despite the punches inflicted, neither man refused to go down. Knowing that Redwine was unarmed and might possibly lose the fight, Parsley pulled a four-barrel pepperbox pistol out of his side pocket. He shouted, "I will shoot your God damned heart out of you."

Then, in a cowardly act, Parsley fired two shots in quick succession. There was a brief pause before a third shot was heard. As the third bullet entered Redwine's stomach, he cried out, "Father, I have been shot."

Pepperbox pistol similar to the one Parsley used to kill James Redwine. *Public domain.*

As the crowd gathered around, Johnson confronted Parsley, "Dick, you should be ashamed of shooting the neighborhood boys." Parsley responded, "God damn him, he shot me!" He was not shot, and all witnesses testified that Redwine was unarmed during the struggle.

Redwine's sixty-seven-year-old father watched the scene unfold before his eyes. After his son was shot, he stumbled about seventy yards before his son fell into his arms. With all the strength he had, they tried to make it for home. They made it twenty-five yards before James couldn't go any further. Johnson and Lowry came to his aid, and they were able to get the younger Redwine to his house.

Drs. Rooker and Silvey came to Redwine's residence. Dr. Rooker examined the wound and remarked that the round could not be retrieved. Redwine remained silent about the shooting. His last words were "I am not long for this world; I have got a dead shot." James Redwine was pronounced dead at ten o'clock on Christmas morning. Parsley had fled the scene, and his whereabouts were unknown.

After the testimony of the witnesses, the jury found that James Redwine was killed by Dick Parsley, and Parsley was charged with second-degree murder. Squire Cropper, the justice of the peace for Delaware Township, issued a warrant for Parsley's arrest.

The community was outraged by the senseless murder, that a life was worth less than a Christmas turkey. But what enraged people even more than the murder was that the murderer was allowed to walk free. Parsley hung around town for a few hours, likely to say goodbye to his wife, Mary. They had been married for only six months. Parsley fled to Kentucky, where he still had family.

The citizens wondered if justice would be served. Sentiment within the community was that Coroner Loehr was the only one with enough integrity to pursue justice. Dr. Loehr was not one to back down from anyone. As coroner, he once arrested a colleague, Dr. A.C. Freeman, for performing an abortion. The doctor vowed to kill Dr. Loehr on first sight.

The funeral of James Redwine was held the day after the inquest. The service, held at the Heady cemetery, was attended by many in the community. Redwine was a Civil War veteran. He enlisted in Company I of the 153rd Indiana Infantry regiment. The unit was only in service from March to September 1865 but saw some action in Kentucky months after Robert E. Lee surrendered at Appomattox in April.

It is hard for a father to watch his son die, but perhaps the hardest hit was his family. He left behind a wife, Nancy, and five children who all depended on him for support.

As the search continued for Parsley, people began to point the finger as to who was to blame for his escape. How was he able to walk away from a crowd of neighbors? Why were those neighbors and friends making little effort to apprehend Redwine's killer?

But their anger was eventually directed at the politicians of the state. Citizens blamed the laws of Indiana for encouraging the heartless spirit of the people. Officers must capture criminals at their own expense and receive nothing for their labor. Sheriffs and constables were seldom allowed expenses to hunt escaped criminals. There was outrage that no reward was offered for the apprehension of Parsley.

Six weeks after the murder, Parsley was arrested in Kentucky and brought back to Noblesville to stand trial. His trial was scheduled to begin during the April 1876 term. He hired an Indianapolis attorney, Major J.W. Gordon, to defend him.

Gordon's reputation throughout the state of Indiana was well known. Besides his famed career as a litigator, he had served in the Indiana House of Representatives, rising to the post of Speaker; enlisted in the Mexican

Grave of James Redwine, located in Heady Cemetery in the Sunblest neighborhood. *Author's collection*.

American War; and then reenlisted during the Civil War, rising to the rank of major.

At the time that Parsley hired Gordon to represent him, the major's name was being thrown around as a possible gubernatorial candidate or state attorney general.

Milford Parsley pleaded not guilty by reason of self-defense. But his experienced attorney was not able to save him. He was found guilty and sentenced to prison for two years for the killing of James Redwine.

Upon his release from prison, he reunited with his wife. The Parsleys moved to Noblesville and started a family, and Milford held various jobs until his death in 1911.

Fishers Station, which had just become a town three years earlier, experienced its first homicide. But in a few years, this incident would pale in comparison to what would eventually befall the town.

14

ROBBERY OF THE FISHERS NATIONAL BANK

I attribute my life of crime to a yellow streak I have had all my life.
—William Ryan at his sentencing for his second bank robbery.

When the Fishers National Bank opened its doors on July 8, 1913, residents were overcome with a sense of pride in their community. Centrally located in the business district of Fishers, it was equipped with all the modern-day conveniences that one would expect for its patrons. It may not have been the largest bank in Hamilton County, but for the first time, residents no longer had to go to Noblesville, Castleton or Indianapolis to do their banking. The bank came to symbolize the growth and progress of Fishers.

The bank was a federally chartered institution, which differed from state banks. At the close of the Civil War, the government passed the National Banking Act of 1863. The act set out to establish a national banking system through the creation of privately owned banks chartered by the federal government. Banks would issue their own currency, printed by the federal government. The currency would look almost identical except for the name of the issuing bank. With many banks folding during this time, the banking act hoped to create a safe, sound and reliable banking and monetary system.

Each national bank was given a unique charter number in order of its creation. When the Fishers National Bank was issued its charter number, 10419, the bank joined the ranks of the thousands of other national banks across the United States. The bank's creation came exactly fifty years after

Banknote of the Fishers National Bank. Featured on the bill is Hugh McCulloch, U.S. Treasury secretary. *Public domain.*

Indiana's first national bank, the First National Bank of Fort Wayne, Charter No. 11, established in 1863.

Although Fishers was a small rural town, the bank was not immune from those who tried to get money the easy way. One of the first crimes the bank encountered was in 1915, when seventy-eight-year-old ex-convict George Pope secured a $300 loan by presenting forged documents identifying himself as Benjamin Smith, a wealthy farmer. Circuit court judge Meade Vestal sentenced the elderly man to state prison for two to fourteen years, essentially giving him a death sentence.

In addition to these financial crimes, a crime epidemic of a different variety was sweeping the country, manifesting itself in the form of daytime bank robberies and nighttime burglaries. The bank boasted its modern double door vault in newspaper advertisements. Patrons were assured that their money was "double" safe within its secured vault.

The vault was put to the test in February 1920. Five burglars broke in during the night and successfully burned through the outer door of the bank vault. When they came to the inner door, they were not as successful. After they gave up trying to break into the safe, they broke into something a little easier, three safe deposit boxes. They escaped with three revolvers, seven cents and a typewriter, swiped from the cashier's desk. The vault did its job, and the money was safe. Within just a few months, the safe would be returned from the factory, where it was fixed, and any evidence that there was a burglary was all but gone.

The 1920s saw a rise in organized crime as citizens came to terms with Prohibition. The number of bank robberies continued to rise across the

United States. Then on October 29, 1929, the Great Depression struck, which further added to the rising crime epidemic. Law enforcement was severely understaffed, which led the State Banking Association to form vigilante committees in almost every county to assist in the apprehension of the suspects. These ordinary citizens were imbued with police powers and the authorization to use deadly force if necessary to capture lawbreakers. A reward would be given for the capture, dead or alive.

It had been ten years since the bank was burglarized, and as cities and states grappled with the problem of bank robberies, Fishers was able to avoid it—that was, until the morning of Monday, February 24, 1930. The robbery would have major consequences, not just for the suspects, but for the future of the bank itself.

The morning started off just like any other. Eighteen-year-old Vera Mollenkopf was working the counter while twenty-one-year-old Sadie Woods was the acting cashier. A.P Butz, who served as the cashier of the bank from 1923 to 1930, injured his eye and was out of work for a few days.

At 11:15 a.m., a green Chevrolet sedan occupied by three men pulled up to the bank. Two of the men entered the bank. One of them approached Woods to make change for a dollar. As she proceeded to make change, both men drew pistols and ordered both young women into the vault.

They grabbed as much as they could, making off with $2,000 in cash and $10,000 in negotiable bonds. In their hurried attempt to get the women into the vault, they overlooked $1,750 in cash that had been knocked on the floor.

The two men raced back to the car and sped off down Main Street (116th Street). It wasn't going to be an easy getaway, as two vehicles loaded with Fishers residents pursued the bank robbers. The chase continued for a couple of miles. The posse, who were all unarmed, made the decision to terminate the chase as the suspect vehicle fled south on Allisonville Road, back toward Indianapolis.

The next day, police unexpectedly got their first break in the case. Indianapolis police officers Otis Baker and C.O. Johnson were called to 45 South West Street, a restaurant owned by Bud Pendergraw. Thirty-year-old William Bryant, who lived in an apartment directly above the restaurant, was intoxicated and causing a disturbance with another patron, John Barleycorn. Officers placed Bryant under arrest for public intoxication.

As they were leaving, Bryant took a small package out of his pocket and discarded it on the table. The officers retrieved it and proceeded to examine its contents. Inside the package, they discovered $3,600 in bonds and securities. Specifically, a $500 and $10 Liberty bond; $1,000 Chicago,

Fishers Bank robbery suspect, William Bryant, aka William Ryan. Later convicted of federal bank robbery in Kentucky. *From the* Indianapolis News, *February 27, 1930.*

Milwaukee, St. Paul & Pacific Railroad bond; a $1,000 Norwegian Hydro-Electric Nitrogen Corporation bond; and three shares of stock in the Fishers National Bank.

Based on this discovery, the officers searched Bryant's apartment and recovered another $1,600 in stock certificates and $75 in cash. A .45-caliber pistol, which had been reported stolen from the bank, was also found. Bryant was charged with vagrancy and held at the Marion County Jail on a $10,000 bond.

Because of Bryant's intoxication, detectives had to wait until the next day to question him. A sober Bryant wasn't much better, as he refused to answer any questions other than to say that he was innocent. He had already been positively identified by the two bank tellers.

Hamilton County sheriff Thomas Ramsey had Bryant brought back to the county to await trial. Every method was employed to get Bryant to talk, but he still refused to name any of his accomplices. Even a reduced sentence from life imprisonment wasn't enticing enough to reveal his co-conspirators.

Bryant's refusal to talk made it difficult for Sheriff Ramsey to investigate his background. But a clearer picture started to develop after he received a letter from the superintendent of the Indiana State Penal Farm in Putnamville. Bryant was not his real name. That was an alias, and his real name was William Ryan. He had originally served time there from June to November 1929 on a blind tiger charge. While at the penal farm, Ryan told authorities he was born in Tulsa, Oklahoma, and he was part Indian.

The sheriff received credible evidence that friends of Ryan's were planning to break him out of jail. A conference was held between Sheriff Ramsey; Emmett Fertig, county prosecutor; and Detective Chauncey Manning of the newly formed Bureau of Criminal Identification to try Ryan on March 24 instead of waiting until the April term. Judge Fred T. Hines would preside over the trial.

Leading up to the trial, security at the jail was tight. Two of the nine prisoners, including Ryan, were held in solitary confinement. They were not allowed to be outside, and they were under guard even while they bathed.

The morning of the scheduled trial, Ryan's attorney, Clyde Miller, requested a continuance because they were not prepared. Judge T.E. Kane, filling in for Judge Hines, who was out for an illness, granted the continuance until March 28.

William Ryan surprised the court the morning of his trial when he agreed to plead guilty to bank robbery. Ryan's statement to the court was that he took full blame for his actions and he had no ill feeling toward the officers or the court. Judge Kane sentenced Ryan to the Indiana State Prison for ten years, the max allowed under Indiana law. Ryan would eventually name his two accomplices.

Edinburg is a small town about fifty miles south of Fishers. In the Haslam pool room, the town marshal, George Snyder, at the request of Chauncey Manning, arrested a local resident, Wilbur Ferguson, in connection to the bank robbery of the Fishers National Bank.

Wilbur Ferguson was well known in Edinburg but not for the better. He had been arrested occasionally for assault over the years. Most recently, he was arrested for selling a half pint of white mule whiskey in violation of

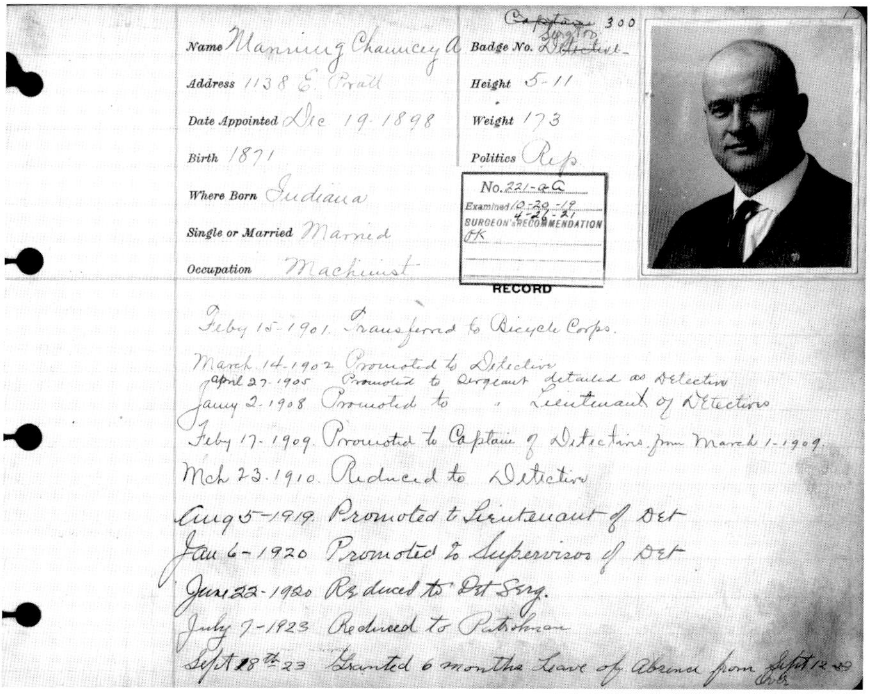

Name Manning Chauncey A
Badge No. 300
Address 1138 E. Pratt
Height 5-11
Date Appointed Dec 19-1898
Weight 173
Birth 1871
Politics Rep.
Where Born Indiana
Single or Married Married
Occupation Machinist

No. 221-a-G
Examined 10-20-19 4-26-21
SURGEON'S RECOMMENDATION
OK

RECORD

Feby 15-1901. Transferred to Bicycle Corps.
March 14-1902 Promoted to Detective
April 27-1905 Promoted to Sergeant detailed as Detective
Jany 2-1908 Promoted to Lieutenant of Detectives
Feby 17-1909. Promoted to Captain of Detectives from March 1-1909.
Mch 23-1910. Reduced to Detective
Aug 5-1919. Promoted to Lieutenant of Det
Jan 6-1920 Promoted to Supervisor of Det
June 22-1920 Reduced to Det Serg.
July 7-1923 Reduced to Patrolman
Sept 18th 23 Granted 6 months Leave of Absence from Sept 12-23
Over

Indianapolis Police personnel record of Detective Chauncey Manning. *Indianapolis Public Library*.

Prohibition statutes. Ferguson was taken to the Johnson County Jail to await extradition back to Hamilton County.

Upon arrival at the Hamilton County Jail, he was placed in a cell next to William Ryan, who was waiting to be transported to the Indiana State Prison. Both men claimed to not know each other when they met face to face. Ferguson also claimed to have no connection with the robbery, but like Ryan, he was positively identified by the bank tellers.

A few days after his arrest and after about eighteen hours of continuous questioning, Ferguson broke and admitted his involvement in the bank robbery. An hour later, he was sentenced to ten years in the Indiana State Prison by Judge Kane.

After Ferguson originally told authorities that he burned his portion of the money, he confessed that he traded it to a secondhand store in exchange for clothes and cash. Once the authorities were able to get them back in their possession, $9,000 had already been recovered. With two suspects sentenced, attention went toward identifying the third suspect and the recovery of the remaining bonds and cash.

It only took a couple of days before the last of the trio was captured. Cecil Johnson was arrested in a sting operation on Massachusetts Avenue by Indianapolis Police detectives and Chauncey Manning. Johnson was identified as the mastermind behind the robbery and the getaway driver.

Cecil Johnson had an extensive criminal record, and this wasn't his first bank robbery. At the age of eighteen, he joined a criminal gang headed by Mamie Isley, referred to as the "queen." Johnson, along with six others, robbed the Alert State Bank in Decatur of $45,000 in May 1922. The gang led by Isley used armor-plated automobiles equipped with machine guns. It was Johnson who turned state's evidence and led to the conviction of all the gang members, including Mamie Isley. His testimony brought an end to one of the "biggest bank robbing and safe cracking syndicates" that has ever operated in Indiana. For his testimony, Johnson was sentenced to the Indiana State Prison for two years.

Just like Ryan and Ferguson, Cecil Johnson pled guilty to bank robbery and was sentenced to a ten-year term in the Indiana State Prison. Although he was the last of the trio to be caught, he was still willing to provide the authorities with valuable information. He confessed that they were all part of a gang of bank robbers that had plans to rob banks across Indiana. He provided names that led to arrests of other bank robbers.

With the case officially closed, the Fishers National Bank still faced some challenges. Although most of the money was recovered, the economic

Fishers Bank robbery suspects Cecil Johnson (*left*) and Wilbur Ferguson (*right*). *From the* Indianapolis Star, *April 6, 1930.*

depression took its toll on the bank. A little more than a month after the robbery, the bank officially closed its doors on March 31.

The portion of the bonds that were not recovered during the robbery ended up as a lawsuit against the cashier of the bank. A.P. Butz was the guardian of Glenn Lyle, a Civil War veteran. Butz had invested $850 of Lyle's estate in unregistered Liberty bonds. Those bonds were taken during the robbery and never recovered. The court held that Butz, as guardian, was liable for the loss. The case was appealed to the Indiana Supreme Court.

Butz claimed that he took reasonable measures to protect Lyle's estate and therefore should not be held liable. The Indiana Supreme Court disagreed and sided with the circuit court's decision. Since other Liberty bonds that had been registered were recovered, it was negligence on the part of Butz, and he was required to reimburse the estate.

The former Fishers National Bank. *Larry A. Reynolds.*

In 1934, the Fishers National Bank was purchased by Fred Appel for $1,000. He owned the Fishers Lumber Company, and his hope was to bring another bank back to Fishers. That didn't happen, and instead it was turned into a restaurant.

The fate of the three suspects in the Indiana State Prison took an ironic twist. Wilbur Ferguson had been sick for a couple of years and spent most of the time in the infirmary. He was diagnosed with tuberculosis and the parole board decided to grant him parole in May 1935.

Cecil Johnson had been a model prisoner, and as a reward he was sent to the honor farm, where prisoners are allowed a little bit more freedom. But Johnson wanted more freedom than what was provided. On August 7, 1936, Johnson, along with one other prisoner, escaped.

William Ryan was granted parole on September 3, 1936. The prosecutor at the time, Emmet Fertig, was now the mayor of Noblesville, and he urged against Ryan's parole. But it was Ryan's cooperation in identifying his accomplices that helped to secure his release.

In less than a year, Ryan would be involved in another robbery in Kentucky. After his release, he met up with an ex-convict, Earl Wines, who he had met while they were both incarcerated at the Indiana State Prison. Wines had been sentenced for robbing the Union Trust Company bank in Indianapolis in 1926. He was released about a year before Ryan.

On June 17, 1937, Ryan participated in robbing the People's Bank in Dunnville, Kentucky. Ryan and another accomplice, Marion Hart, escaped into the woods. Earl Wines was captured, and he identified his accomplices immediately. A posse led by Lincoln County sheriff H.S.

Anderson actively hunted for the suspects. Ryan was arrested the next day near the town of Arabia.

It would be a couple of months before Hart would be located. In the meantime, Wines and Ryan were held in Louisville, Kentucky.

During Ryan's time in prison, a major piece of federal legislation was passed that would change the way his trial would be handled from his first trial in Hamilton County. In response to the Great Depression and the thousands of bank failures across the country, Franklin Roosevelt created the Federal Deposit Insurance Corporation (FDIC). This independent agency was formed to promote public confidence in the U.S. financial system by ensuring that depositors' money was secure.

When Ryan and his co-conspirators robbed the Fishers National Bank, bank robbery was a state crime tried in circuit court. When Ryan robbed the People's Bank in Kentucky, the bank was a member of the FDIC and therefore the crime was under the jurisdiction of the federal government.

U.S. Commissioner Ray H. Kirchdorfer ordered a federal grand jury to hear the case. On October 15, 1937, all three suspects were found guilty in federal court. Hart was sentenced to fifteen years, and Ryan and Wines both received seventeen years each. The trio were sent to the Atlanta Federal Penitentiary to live out their sentence.

In 1944, Cecil Johnson was found living in Adams County, Iowa. After escaping prison, he fled to Texas for three years before settling down in Iowa as a farmer. While in Iowa, he registered with the Chicago draft board. When he failed to report for induction on November 29, 1943, FBI agents traced him to Iowa. Johnson eluded them before they arrived. Johnson had enough and returned to Indianapolis to surrender to the clemency board in the hopes of wiping the slate clean.

Because Johnson was married with a couple of children and had been living an "exemplary" life since his escape, the clemency board granted him a release from the remainder of his sentence. Since he no longer had to hide, he moved his family back to Indianapolis. He lived the remainder of his life within the law before passing away at the age of seventy-eight.

Wilbur Ferguson moved back to Edinburg and continued to live in ill health for many years. He died on April 3, 1953.

15

THE MURDER OF CONSTABLE FRANK CAREY

His Sun has gone down while it was yet Day.
—eulogy spoken at Frank Carey's funeral, June 10, 1900

The morning of Saturday, June 9, 1900, residents throughout Hamilton County had already heard of the awful tragedy that occurred the evening before in the small Quaker town of Carmel. A fight broke out in the peaceful village and left two people dead. Among them was Frank Carey, the first police officer killed in the line of duty in Hamilton County. Fishers Station would soon be called upon to assist in the investigation, the first of its kind.

At the turn of the century, Carmel was a small town of about eight hundred people. The Quakers founded the city, which was originally called Bethlehem. When the post office was established, another town in Indiana had already laid claim to the name, so the town became known as Carmel. Because of the Quaker influence, the town had a reputation as one of the quietest and most orderly towns in Indiana.

Carmel's reputation took a huge hit when a traveling evangelist came to town about three months before and started causing trouble. Thomas Jefferson Johnson, commonly known as "Cyclone Johnson" or the "Kentucky Cyclone," claimed to be a man of God, but most people thought just the opposite. An editorial in the *Hamilton County Ledger* described Johnson has being as vicious in nature and at heart while playing the part of the "evangelist" while living the role of crook and gambler. He "stole the livery of heaven to serve the devil in."

Cyclone Johnson was born in Jackson County, Kentucky, in 1868. His childhood wasn't the best, and from the age of eight, he was forced to raise himself. Around his eighteenth birthday, he moved to Moral, Indiana, in Shelby county. After a couple of years, he moved a little farther south, settling in Boggstown, also in Shelby County. It wasn't long before Johnson was arrested for stealing a horse. In 1888, he was sent to the Indiana State Prison in Jeffersonville.

After he served his prison term, Johnson seemed to settle down. He got married in 1890 and eventually had four boys ranging in age from three to nine. The family lived for a few years in Covington, Kentucky, right across the river from Cincinnati. It was in Covington that Johnson was "converted" to religion and so began his career as a preacher. Johnson moved his family in 1898, when he would take his sermon preaching to the streets of Indianapolis.

There were many people who were attracted to Johnson's style of preaching. But it also aroused disdain and hatred in others. Most preachers were concerned with preaching acceptance and forgiveness and teaching individuals to lead a life devoid of sin, but Johnson was concerned with none of that. He used the pulpit to further his political agenda and slander public officials. He even denounced ministers of other churches and believed that he was preaching the Bible as he understood it.

Shortly after arriving in Indianapolis, he directed his attacks at Indianapolis mayor Thomas Taggart, along with other public officials. He accused them of dishonesty and using their offices for the furtherance of crime. Mayor Taggart was already on his third term as mayor. He was widely regarded as the political boss of the Democratic Party in Indiana and would go on to chair the Democratic National Committee.

Johnson's directed attacks against the city administration attracted the ire of the local police force. Johnson was arrested time after time for obstructing the streets and fined multiple times. At the time of his death, he still had fines that were unpaid. The corner of Washington Street and Kentucky Avenue was a favorite spot of Johnson's, and he preached his sermons from a small pulpit that he would wheel around town.

Johnson's followers believed that he was being persecuted by the police. Every time he was arrested, he became a martyr for his cause, and that undoubtedly earned him new followers. The intensity of his abuse toward the police increased with each arrest.

During the summer of 1899, Johnson and his followers had circulated a flyer around Indianapolis that angered almost everyone. The language in the flyer attacked every class and race of people in Indianapolis as well the police, city officials and other ministers. For a few days, Johnson was barred from preaching. Upon a promise to cease the attacks, he was allowed to resume his public speaking. But a fiery preacher like Cyclone Johnson was unable to keep that promise and was arrested once again.

His followers routinely paid his fines, but this latest arrest started to erode their respect for him. His time in Indianapolis had come to an end. Johnson made the decision to move his family to Carmel.

His time in Carmel began cordially, and he had been welcomed into many of the churches around town. But it didn't take long before that welcome was rescinded. Johnson had a certain charisma, and within a few months, he had acquired a new set of followers.

A tent was set up on the west side of town, and Johnson was back to his normal style of preaching. He accused highly respected people in the community of either adultery or fornication, naming them specifically in his sermons. He would say any number of things that were hateful and without any credible evidence to back up the accusations.

As the only source of income for the family, business was good. An admission fee of ten cents, charged only on the weekends, always kept his tents full. People were known to loiter outside the tent, which infuriated Johnson. He believed that if they wanted to listen to the sermon, they should pay. There were others who cared nothing about the sermons but were there to heckle the street preacher.

Cyclone Johnson had many enemies in Carmel. The weekend before the murder of Frank Carey, Johnson requested constables to guard his tent for protection. All was quiet for a few days until Thursday, June 7. A local resident, Elmer Cass, showed up at Johnson's tent with the intent to arouse anger in the hostile preacher. It didn't take long before Johnson assaulted Cass for interrupting his sermon. This wasn't the first time that Johnson resorted to anger. Years earlier, he admitted to shooting a man but had since been reformed.

Elmer Cass went to the home of Carmel's justice of the peace, Squire Collins, and a warrant was issued for Cyclone Johnson for assault and battery. On the morning of Friday, June 8, Johnson boarded an electric streetcar for Indianapolis. The rumor had spread that he was going to Indianapolis to get a supply of ammunition. Johnson felt that people were out to hurt or kill him, and he wanted to be better prepared.

While in Indianapolis, he met up with an old friend, Albert Cross. Cross was a street vendor from Carmel who had also been deputized when Johnson requested police protection. Johnson confided in Cross about the threats against his life, and he knew that he could be arrested at any time.

Johnson showed Cross a small penknife and dirk that he always carried with him. But he also told Cross that he was better prepared for trouble because he had recently acquired a revolver and ammunition and if trouble was renewed, he would be ready.

It was shortly before 4:00 p.m. when a friend of Johnson's, Clinton Gue, gave him a ride back to Carmel. He was home for about an hour before there was a knock on the door. Johnson opened the door, and standing before him was township constable Ed Carey and his cousin, Frank Carey, who had just been deputized minutes earlier.

Constable Frank Carey, first law enforcement officer killed in Hamilton County. *Carmel-Clay Historical Society.*

Constables are like marshals in that they both have arrest powers. But where they differed was constables were elected by the townships while marshals were either elected or appointed in the different localities. Ed Carey was the elected constable for Clay Township.

Frank Carey was a well-respected member of the Carmel community. His father, Lemuel Carey, was one of the county commissioners. Frank Carey, along with his wife and children, lived on a 160-acre farm about two miles northwest of Carmel in an area known as Poplar Ridge. Frank Carey had graduated from Earlham College and was a member of the Masons and Knights of Pythias. He returned to Carmel, where he worked as a farmer. He had one of the largest farms in the area, consisting of 10 horses, 12 head of cattle, 100 hogs, 225 sheep and over 60 acres of corn. At the time of his death, it was one of the largest public auction sales anywhere in the county.

Carey was also active in local politics. In 1892, he was elected as a state delegate by the Clay Township Mass Convention for Republicans. In 1899, he served as a juror during the Tyler Marion lynching case that occurred in Scott County. The trial was held in U.S. federal court in Indianapolis. Tyler Marion had been arrested for the attempted murder of his wife. A lynch mob broke into the jail and lynched Marion before he could be tried. Marion's father brought a lawsuit in federal court. The jury awarded the father $5 for damages, not the $5,000 requested, but it was the moral victory that people celebrated. It made it clear that vigilante mobs were murderers and that sheriffs had a duty to protect prisoners in its custody.

Carey was returning home from Indianapolis when his cousin, Ed, called him to assist with arresting Cyclone Johnson. Since Frank Carey was a farmer by trade, Ed deputized him so that he would be legally protected when they arrested Johnson. The thought of his family probably went through his mind, especially his twin boys, Wyatt and Lemuel, born just six months earlier on New Year's Day.

Cyclone Johnson willingly went with the Careys, but his only request was that they provide him protection, as there were many people threatening him harm. The trio went to the livery stables owned by Jackson Jefferies for a preliminary trial in front of Squire Collins. Johnson argued that the case was being tried too fast and he needed time to prepare his defense. Collins agreed, and the decision was made to continue the trial until Monday, when they would reconvene in Johnson's tent.

Word reached Johnson's followers that he had been arrested, and they immediately swarmed the proceedings. At the turn of the century, the justice system in Hamilton County operated a lot differently. Elmer Cass had hired his own prosecuting attorney, David W. Patty.

David Patty was a longtime resident of Carmel and lived within Delaware Township before the boundary lines were redrawn separating Clay and Delaware Townships at the White River. Patty was hard and a little rough around the edges. He fought in the Civil War, having served in Company A of the Fifth Indiana Volunteer Cavalry regiment. He was interned seven weeks in the Andersonville Prison in Georgia as a prisoner of war. After the war, he served as sheriff of Hamilton County from 1870 to 1872 and then joined the Hamilton County bar as a practicing lawyer. He would eventually become one of Hamilton County's prosecuting attorneys.

Patty, seizing on the opportunity to do some grandstanding before the judge and Johnson's followers, delivered a speech. The *Hamilton County Ledger* described the speech as an attempt to restore peace by urging both sides to be quiet and not cause trouble.

Patty's speech rubbed Johnson the wrong way, and Johnson, addressing Patty, shouted, "Shut your damn mouth or I will shut it for you." Not one to be intimidated, Patty continued to speak.

Patty recalled that Squire Collins stepped in between them. At some point, Johnson's friend Clinton Gue raised something in the air. Patty was unsure if it was a gun. As the crowd moved in, Johnson struck Patty on the left side of the face.

A struggle ensued amid the crowd, with Johnson's followers on one side and those wanting to see justice administered on the other. Johnson pulled out a revolver and fired twice before running to the rear of the stable. Frank Carey was in pursuit.

As they entered a back room, Carey tripped, causing both him and Johnson to fall to the floor. Johnson fired two rounds at Frank Carey. As Johnson stood up in the doorway, someone in the crowd drew a revolver and shot Johnson.

After the shooting had subsided, Johnson lay on the floor motionless. Frank Carey was severely wounded but conscious. While Ed Carey was holding his head, Frank muttered his last words, "Send for Dr. Hershey." A few seconds later, Frank Carey breathed his last breath.

Both men were dead, lying inches from each other, by the time that Dr. Hershey arrived. One of Johnson's loyal followers, Martin Long, was injured in the right wrist during the shooting. He had an arterial bleed, and as Dr. Hershey applied pressure to stop the bleeding, he told Long to accompany him to his office so that he could dress the wound. They made it a short distance before Long raced back to the stable. Standing over Johnson's dead body, he pulled out a large knife from his pocket. Knowing the killer of Cyclone Johnson was somewhere in the crowd, he set down a challenge, exclaiming, "Damn you, you have killed him. I am game, come on." He was eventually persuaded to put the knife down and leave with Dr. Hershey.

Frank Carey's body was taken to his home. An external examination showed that he was shot twice. He was struck in the thigh and on the left side of the neck, severing the jugular vein. Johnson was shot three times with the bullets grouped together near his left breast. Any one of the bullets could have penetrated his heart.

Johnson's funeral service was held on Monday morning, at his residence, mainly attended by his family and followers. It was officiated by Reverend Eddie Cosler of Indianapolis. His remains were taken to Crown Hill cemetery.

Frank Carey's funeral was held on Sunday afternoon at the Friends Church in Carmel. People from all over the county and surrounding areas came to pay their respects. The Carey family was well respected, and this tragedy shook the small town to its core. The eulogy spoke of Carey's Christian principles, his devotion to God and his unending love for his wife, Hattie, and his children. His body was buried in the Carmel cemetery.

The investigation into the murder of Frank Carey began the very next day. Squire J.M. Stipp, justice of the peace for Fishers Station, assisted by Dr. F.A. Tucker, were called upon to hold the inquest, as Squire Collins was now a witness to the incident. Ten witnesses had been interviewed before the investigation was suspended. Rumor had circulated that several of Johnson's brothers were coming to Carmel from Kentucky to avenge his death. After the rumor was dispelled, the investigation continued Tuesday morning.

The first step in the investigation was to determine who killed Frank Carey and Cyclone Johnson. Followers of Johnson claimed that Frank Carey was actually shot by Ed Carey. Because of the accusation, friends and family wanted a postmortem examination to disprove that Frank Carey was shot by Ed. It was finally agreed upon that based on the position of the two men, the nature of the wound and the range of the bullets, that Carey was shot by Johnson. A postmortem examination was not completed.

Attention now turned toward who killed Cyclone Johnson. Of all the witnesses interviewed, not one person could or would say who shot him. Prosecutor Patty was asked his opinion as to who shot Johnson.

His response was typical of most everyone else: "I am unable to say as there were several men between me and the fellow who used the revolver.

Carmel police statue, tribute to Constable Frank Carey, erected not far from where he was killed. *Author's collection.*

However, I might say, I am satisfied who did the shooting but I have no positive knowledge on the subject."

Knowing that no one would come forward to tell the truth or present evidence about the identity of the shooter, Squire Stipp submitted the final report to the Hamilton County prosecutor. The official findings were that Frank Carey was killed by Cyclone Johnson and Johnson's assailants are unknown.

The awful tragedy destroyed two families and ripped apart a community. Hattie Carey was now a widow with six-month-old twins who would never know their father. Their oldest son, age eleven, grieved in private so he would not burden his mother with any more sorrow. She eventually moved in with her in-laws, and Lemuel Carey put the farm up for public sale.

Across town, the Johnson family was grieving also. Three-year-old Chester Johnson was being entertained by his three older brothers while the body of their father lay in the parlor. The young widow, who hadn't slept in two days, had to carry on for the sake of her children. She would remember him as a martyr for his religion.

The town of Carmel was dealing with a tragedy that it had never faced. But the strong Quaker faith of the residents taught them to deal with it with humility and forgiveness. Rumors swirled in the weeks after the killing that Johnson's followers were run out of town, but that was far from the truth. Everyone agreed that Johnson was the aggressor, but they refused to hold his friends responsible for his misdeeds. Residents comforted Johnson's widow and children in the weeks after, just as much as they did the Careys.

Frank Carey's law enforcement career lasted only a couple of hours, but his impact and legacy as Hamilton County's first officer killed in the line of duty is still remembered to this day.

16
THE PHARMACIST WHO SOLD MORE THAN DRUGS

It also makes it unlawful for any druggist or pharmacist to sell, barter or give away intoxicating liquor except on the written prescription of a reputable physician engaged in active practice of his profession.
—Blind Tiger Law 1907

There wasn't one person in Fishers Station who didn't know Allen Harrison. He was well-respected and operated the town's only pharmacy; his store was one of the oldest in Fishers. The store was originally owned by Wiley Dixon, who operated a grocery store and was one of the first merchants in town, even before the arrival of Sam Trittipo. The store changed ownership five times before it was eventually sold to Harrison in 1893. Once Harrison took possession, he converted it from a grocery store to a drugstore and remodeled it with all of the modern conveniences. He even had assistance from Dan Socks, town marshal; Dr. Alexander, before his reputation took a downward turn; and Squire Bolton, the town's justice of the peace. While many residents visited the store for their prescriptions, apparently that wasn't the only thing he sold.

Fights were not an uncommon thing in Fishers, especially when alcohol was involved. So that probably made it unusual when three men, Sherman Mason, William Hodgin and John Moose, got into a fight inside Harrison's drugstore in January 1907. Moose took the brunt of the beating and was arrested and tried for intoxication. Hodgin and Mason were charged with assault and battery.

Cassius M. Gentry, prosecuting attorney for Hamilton County known for vigorously pursuing cases against saloons. *From the* Noblesville Ledger, *May 2, 1928.*

Newly elected Hamilton County prosecutor Cassius Gentry wasted no time in making examples of the young men, who were regarded as drunks around town. Moose was fined and released and although Hodgin and Mason had the money to pay their fines, they opted to take a jail sentence. It was nothing more than an attempt to make the county pay for their room and board for the ten days they had to serve at the same time denying the county the fine levied against them.

While the two men were locked up in jail, they decided to talk to Prosecutor Gentry about what led up to the fight. They had gone to Harrison's drugstore not to purchase medicine, but something entirely different, whiskey. Although it wasn't out of the ordinary for a pharmacist to provide liquor as long as they had a doctor's prescription, which was common during this period, neither man had a valid prescription.

Liquor consumption was a problem across the entire United States. Beginning in 1900, the Indiana legislature started to pass more restrictive prohibition laws in an attempt to make Indiana "dry." Although a statewide prohibition amendment failed to gain support, legislators were able to pass the "Blind Tiger" law in 1907. A blind tiger was another name for an illegal saloon, and anyone operating one would receive a mandatory jail sentence. This was one of the strictest laws in the country. Between 1900 and 1910, more than 2,500 saloons shut their doors.

The blind tiger law also covered pharmacists who were allowed to sell liquor with a prescription, but it was good for only one sale, and the prescription must be kept on file. Based on the information from Hodgin and Mason, Prosecutor Gentry conducted an investigation. Allen Harrison was eventually charged with six counts under the new blind tiger law for selling liquor without a license and selling liquor in a quantity smaller than a quart without a prescription. Harrison was the first one in Hamilton County charged under the new law, but he was not the only one engaging in the practice.

It would be almost a year before he went on trial. Based on what happened with a restaurant owner in Sheridan later that summer, it possibly foreshadowed what sentence Harrison might be facing. William Franklin was suspected of selling liquor without a license in his restaurant, and Prosecutor Gentry had a search warrant issued. A quart of whiskey was found in Franklin's restaurant and used as evidence in his trial. He was fined fifty dollars and sentenced to thirty days in jail, the minimum sentence under the law. Franklin was the first person convicted under the new blind tiger law in Hamilton County.

The trial was held in circuit court in Noblesville. Hodgin and Mason testified that they purchased whiskey at Harrison's drugstore. Harrison testified that the men came into his store demanding something to drink, and fearing what might happen if he didn't, he gave them something to drink, but it wasn't whiskey. Instead, he gave them Peruna, a patented medicine.

Peruna was a liquid medicine patented by Dr. Samuel Brubaker Hartman from Ohio. It was one of the most popular medicines in the United States. At a cost of one dollar a bottle, it made the doctor a millionaire, as it only cost eighteen cents to produce. He was an amazing salesman and proclaimed that Peruna could cure almost any medical ailment. But the drug's reputation took a hit in 1904 when a reporter wrote an exposé on the miracle drug for *Colliers Weekly* under the headline, "The Great American Fraud." An investigation showed that a bottle of Peruna contained a half of pint of 90 proof alcohol, one and a half pints of water, a flavor cube and a little burned sugar for coloring. The U.S. Bureau of Indian Affairs had already banned the substance on Indian reservations because the bottle was 28 percent alcohol.

Whether Harrison gave them whiskey or Peruna, it didn't really matter, since the result was the same. However, the jury was torn, and after deliberating for two days, they were unable to return a verdict. The jury was evenly split, six to six. The judge dismissed the jury, and Harrison was free.

Although he escaped conviction, his life started to take a downward turn. His pharmacy had already been sold to Arthur West, who turned it into a pool hall and restaurant that eventually would be owned by Vora Trittipo. About six months later, his wife, Clara Harrison, filed for divorce.

They had been married for twenty-three years and had four children: Walter (twenty), Eugene (sixteen), Burton (nine) and Marian (six). She claimed that Harrison had a violent temper and frequently cursed and threatened to kill her and the children. She blamed it on his increasing use of alcohol in the last few years, which makes it all the more plausible that he was selling liquor illegally through his pharmacy. She asked the court for custody of the children and $2,500 in alimony (about $70,000 in 2020). Harrison was wealthy, considering that he owned forty-seven acres in Delaware Township and real estate in Fishers Station, in addition to the proceeds from the sale of the drugstore.

The divorce was probably withdrawn, since she was listed as his spouse on his death certificate. Allen Harrison died less than ten years later at the age of fifty-four, and there is no indication that he ever gave up the whiskey.

BIBLIOGRAPHY

Introduction

Call-Leader (Elwood, IN). "Unusually Muddy." October 21, 1949.

Enterprise (Noblesville, IN). "Early History." May 17, 1907.

Fishers Town Minutes. Ordinance #1. July 21, 1888.

Hamilton County Ledger (Noblesville, IN). "County Capers." May 21, 1897.

———. "Courthouse Column." August 30, 1901.

———. "East Delaware." March 22, 1889.

———. "Olio." September 23, 1898.

Herald (Jasper, IN). "How Did Lickskillet Get Named?" June 23, 1978.

History of Geist Reservoir and Germantown. http://oaklandon.deburger.com/stories/History_of_Geist_Reservoir_and_Germantown.pdf.

Indianapolis News. "Deer Tale Accounts for Name Lickskillet." February 18, 1960.

———. "Town Olio Favored Name of Lickskillet." February 6, 1960.

Nickel Plate Road History. https://www.nickelplatetrail.org/about-the-nickel-plate-trail/history-of-the-trail.

Noblesville Ledger. "50 Years Ago." October 20, 1939.

———. "West Liberty: Gone but Not Forgotten." June 5, 1978.

Reynolds, Larry A. *The Mudsock Scrapbook*. Fishers, IN: Hoosier, Cider Press, 1993.

Shirts, Augustus. *History of Hamilton County, Indiana*. Salem, MA: Higginson Book Company, 1901.

Skinner, Anna. "Supplemental Storage: Citizens Energy Group to Use Retired Quarry as New, 230-Foot Deep Reservoir." *Current in Fishers*, January 21, 2020.

An Illegal Prize Fight

Angola (IN) Herald. "The Roby Cases." March 14, 1894.
Boston Globe. "Fines Only Imposed." August 23, 1894.
———. "Sport Miscellany." January 31, 1894.
Brooklyn (NY) Daily Eagle. "Billy Ernst Knocked Out." December 2, 1896.
Chicago Tribune. "Session of the Heavyweights." August 5, 1900.
Daily Democrat (Huntington, IN). "Gov. Matthews Sustained." June 5, 1895.
———. "The Legislature." March 3, 1893.
———. "Police Stop a Fight." March 17, 1893.
Daily Reporter (Greenwood, IN). "Governor Signs the Boxing Commission Bill." March 11, 1931.
Democrat and Chronicle (Rochester, NY). "A Bloody Prize Fight." October 25, 1893.
Encyclopedia Britannica. "Marquess of Queensbury Rules." https://www.britannica.com/sports/Marquess-of-Queensberry-rules.
Fort Wayne (IN) Sentinel. "Prize Fighting." October 25, 1893.
Hamilton County (IN) Democrat. "Court Proceedings." December 28, 1894.
Indianapolis Journal. "An Early Morning Fight." October 25, 1893.
———. "Fake Sport at Roby." March 7, 1894.
———. "Glove Contests To-Morrow Night." February 26, 1893.
———. "Has Called Out the Militia." September 2, 1893.
———. "Julius-Chomel Commits Suicide in an Illinois-Street Saloon." April 3, 1894.
———. "The Law Vindicated." December 15, 1893.
———. "Requisitions for Prize Fighters." September 27, 1893.
———. "Roby Cases Settled." August 21, 1894.
———. "Roby Trial Begins." December 12, 1893.
———. "Wants to Compromise." October 9, 1893.
Indianapolis News. "Fight Near Broad Ripple." September 19, 1893.
———. "General State News." March 8, 1894.
———. "Seven Terrible Rounds." October 24, 1893.
Indiana State Sentinel. "Roby's Arena Open." June 14, 1893.
Monroeville (IN) Breeze. "Indiana Legislature." January 31, 1895.
Pall Mall Gazette (London, England). "Boxing." February 12, 1895.
Richmond (IN) Item. "Evening Item." June 14, 1893.
South Bend (IN) Tribune. "Calls the Militia." September 2, 1893.

The Ghost of James Payne

Burgess, Joe H. *Hamilton County and the Civil War.* Self-published, 1967.
Fact or Faked: Paranormal Files. Season 1, episode 6. "The Caretaker/Cutter."
Hamilton County Democrat. "Fishers Station." April 8, 1887.
Hamilton County Ledger. "The Death Roll." December 12, 1905.
———. "Wedding Did Not Occur." September 19, 1905.
———. "West Fall Creek." May 13, 1898.
Noblesville Ledger. "Story of West Liberty." September 16, 1939.
U.S. Department of Veteran Affairs. "History of Government Furnished Headstones and Markers." https://www.cem.va.gov/cem/history/hmhist.asp.

The Legend of Heady Hollow

Indianapolis Star. "Ghostly Hoofbeats in Heady Hollow." October 25, 1998.
Noblesville Ledger. "Building Fence on Cement Highway." February 1, 1923.
———. "County Line." November 30, 1964.
———. "Fact or Fiction: The Legends of Heady Hollow." May 21, 1979.
———. "Getting Ready to Fence Cement Road." November 23, 1922.
———. "Hollow's Legendary Land Is Steeped in History." June 4, 1979.

Fall Creek Indian Massacre

Helm, Thomas B. *History of Carroll County, Indiana.*" Chicago: Kingman Brothers, 1882.
Murphy, David Thomas. *Murder in Their Hearts: The Fall Creek Massacre.* Indianapolis: Indiana Historical Society Press, 2010.
Shirts, Augustus Finch. "*A History of Hamilton County, Indiana*." Salem, MA: Higginson Book Company, 1901.
Smith, Oliver H. *Early Indiana Trials and Sketches.* Cincinnati, OH: Moore, Wilstach, Keys & Co., 1858.

JUNCTION 69

Indianapolis News. "Bar Owner Given Ultimatum." February 17, 1981.
———. "Owner Prefers Tavern to Office." October 12, 1978.
Indianapolis Star. "Hamilton County Man Convicted in Shooting." October 2, 1976.
———. "Owner of Topless Bar 'Sick of It'." April 10, 1981.
Noblesville Ledger. "'Bounced' Patrons Fire on Bar, Barely Miss Topless Dancer." March 25, 1981.
———. "Ex-Bar Owner Gets 1–5 Years for Shooting." November 24, 1976.
———. "Fishers Sues Topless Bar." March 4, 1981.
———. "Fishers Tavern Owner Shoots Man." May 16, 1975.
———. "Junction 69 Cited for Zoning Violation as Protestors March." February 12, 1981.
———. "Junction 69 Must Halt Topless or Face Lawsuit." February 17, 1981.
———. "Junction 69 Target of Threats, But Will Reopen, Says Owner." April 4, 1981.
———. "Junction 69 Told to Conform with Zoning." January 23, 1981.
———. "Jury Says Woolum Guilty." October 1, 1976.
———. "No Topless Bar Ordinance Needed: Mayor." December 23, 1980.
———. "Topless Bar's Angry Owner Closes Up Shop." April 8, 1981.
———. "Topless Bar Comes Before Fishers BZA on Feb. 11." February 6, 1981.
———. "Topless Bar Has Federally Guaranteed SBA Loan." February 19, 1981.
———. "Topless Bar 'Technically In Violation' of Zoning." December 5, 1980.
Tipton Daily Tribune. "Illegal Liquor Sales." March 4, 1970.

THE BATTLE OF MUDSOCK

Buffalo (NY) Weekly Express. "A Saloon-Keepers War." November 24, 1881.
Cincinnati Enquirer. "Mudsock." November 25, 1881.
Fort Wayne (IN) Daily Gazette "Morning Gazette." November 24, 1881.
Hamilton County Democrat (Noblesville, IN). "Fishers Station." January 6, 1882.
Indianapolis News. "Affairs at Fishers." December 5, 1881.

Knoxville (TN) Daily Chronicle. "Hostile Hoosiers." November 24, 1881.
Lancaster (PA) Examiner. "Massacre in Indiana." November 30, 1881.
Ledger (Noblesville, IN). "Additional Local." December 9, 1881.
———. "East Delaware." February 3, 1882.
———. "East Delaware." March 24, 1882.
———. "Murder." November 25, 1881.
———. "Temperance." December 15, 1880.
Leeds Mercury (West Yorkshire, England). "Public Ledger." December 10, 1881.
Louisiana Capitolian (Baton Rouge, LA). "Fighting Whiskey." December 3, 1881.
Muncie (IN) Daily Times. "Murdered with a Faucet." November 22, 1881.
New York Times. "A Fight Among Ruffians." November 23, 1881.
Richmond (IN) Item. "Big Fight at Noblesville." November 22, 1881.

A White Cap Beating?

Burlington (VT) Clipper. "White Caps." November 27, 1897.
Hamilton County Democrat. "Klepfer Got Whipped." November 4, 1892.
———. "Minor State Items." March 29, 1889.
———. "Wants a Divorce." October 4, 1889.
———. "White Caps at Lapel." December 27, 1889.
Hamilton County Ledger. "Circuit Court." December 2, 1892.
Indianapolis Journal. "Henry Klepfer Was Drunk." August 6, 1896.
Rogers, Nicholas. *Halloween: From Pagan Ritual to Party Night.* Oxford: Oxford University Press, 2003.
St. Joseph (MO) Gazette-Herald. "White Cap Barbarism." October 29, 1892.

The Mystery of the Eller Bridge Arson

Indianapolis News. "A Beloved Landmark Falls Prey to Wanton Destruction." November 18, 1957.
Noblesville Ledger. "Another Landmark Gone." October 7, 1957.
———. "The County Line." October 9, 1957.
———. "County Officials Inspect Site of Destroyed Bridge." October 11, 1957.

———. "County to Seek Federal Aid to Replace Bridge." October 16, 1957.
———. "8 Bridges Span River in County." September 26, 1969.
———. "Gas Poured on Historic Structure but Motorists Extinguish the Flames." November 9, 1953.
———. "New Bridge Will Cost $500,000 or More, Is Estimate." October 7, 1957.
———. "There Are Nine Bridges Across White River in Hamilton Co." November 9, 1959.
Shirts, Augustus Finch. "*History of Hamilton County Indiana*." Salem, MA: Higginson Book Company, 1901.

THE CITY UNDER THE LAKE

Daily Reporter (Greenfield, IN). "Germantown Lumber Put to Good Use Locally." July 7, 2016.
Griffin, Marjie Gates. *Water Runs Downhill*. Indianapolis: Benham Press, 1981.
Indianapolis News. "City Water Supply." May 23, 1941.
———. "Germantown Loss Rued." April 18, 1958.
———. "Site of Germantown Under Geist Waters." October 24, 1961.
———. "$10,976,042 Left in Geist Estate." September 19, 1939.
———. "Timetable of an Adequate Water Supply." August 9, 1954.
———. "Use of Fall Creek Reservoir Area as State Park Is Considered Again." August 21, 1947.
———. "Water Company Dam Is Approved." April 19, 1941.
Indianapolis Star. "Geist." July 3, 1983.
———. "Submits Low Bid for Dam Project." April 26, 1941.
Noblesville Ledger. "Hamilton Highlights." May 9, 1950.
———. "Hamilton Highlights." June 17, 1950.
———. "Hear Evidence on Fall Creek Township Dam." April 1, 1941.
———. "Ready to Start Work on Dam." May 23, 1941.
Townsend, Andrea. "The History of ISC." https://www.indianapolissailing.org/history.php.

The Grave Robbing Trials of 1903

Dayton (OH) Daily News. "Legal Notice." July 21, 1915.
Hamilton County Democrat (Noblesville, IN). "County News." April 5, 1895.
———. "County News." January 11, 1901.
———. "Did Hampton West Offer to Confess to Grave-Robbing." March 27, 1903.
———. "Ghouls Worked in Many of the Cemeteries of This Co." December 26, 1902.
———. "It Is Called Bunco Steering." February 20, 1903.
———. "New Laws Created by the Present Indiana Legislature." March 20, 1903.
Hamilton County Ledger (Noblesville, IN). "Cantrell Confesses Again." August 11, 1903.
———. "Cantrell Here." March 10, 1903.
———. "Echoes of the West Case." July 21, 1903.
———. "Hampton West Arrested." January 6, 1903.
———. "Shocking Disclosure." October 3, 1902.
———. "The State Rests." July 17, 1903.
———. "Stout May Not be Tried." April 7, 1903.
———. "West Can't Give Bond." January 9, 1903.
———. "West Is on Trial." July 10, 1903.
———. "West Is Sentenced." July 24, 1903.
Indianapolis Journal. "Cantrell on Stage." February 5, 1903.
———. "Caught in the Web." October 1, 1902.
———. "Confessions of a Ghoul." December 2, 1902.
———. "Confession of Ghouls." September 30, 1902.
———. "Ghouls Are Indicted." October 26, 1902.
———. "Ghouls in a Graveyard." September 20, 1902.
———. "Hampton West's Letter." February 1, 1903.
———. "Hampton West Surrenders." December 11, 1902.
———. "Hunting for Bodies." October 3, 1902.
———. "Judge Alford Angry." April 11, 1903.
———. "The Law's Strong Arm." October 2, 1902.
———. "Sanity of Cantrell." February 10, 1903.
———. "State Closes Case." April 22, 1903.
———. "Three Men Arrested." February 24, 1901.
———. "Walked into a Trap." January 5, 1903.
Indianapolis News. "Adolph Asch, on Police Force for 26 Years, Is Dead." December 29, 1914.

———. "Cantrell Defended on Plea of Insanity." April 20, 1903.
———. "Cantrell's Marriage Starts Trouble Anew." December 24, 1915.
———. "Cantrell Tells of Fight." March 14, 1903.
———. "Crown Hill's Origin and Development." July 9, 1910.
———. "Colored Bartender Beaten." October 23, 1900.
———. "Defense Is Hit Hard by Court." February 4, 1903.
———. "Dr. Jos. Alexander Egged." October 31, 1903.
———. "Farmers Burned the Men in Effigy." April 23, 1903.
———. "Fired on Ghouls." March 14, 1903.
———. "Hampton West Buried at Fishers Station." August 29, 1904.
———. "Heart Disease Fatal to Chauncey Manning." November 5, 1932.
———. "Silken Shroud Before the Jury." February 6, 1903.
———. "Two Bloodhounds." December 25, 1893.
———. "Woman's Skeleton Is Found in Attic." April 26, 1920.
Indianapolis Star. "How Group Insurance Works." December 7, 1925.
———. "Manning Gives Up Patrolman's Berth." October 10, 1923.
Jasper (IN) Weekly Courier. "The Cadaver Traffic." February 13, 1903.
———. "Stolen Human Bodies." October 17, 1902.
Morning Post (Raleigh, NC). "Told by a Ghoul." July 12, 1903.
Pittsburgh Press. "A Woman Saw Two Murders." August 10, 1903.
Richmond (IN) Item. "Asch Arrested for Evading Military." October 19, 1909.
Scranton (PA) Truth. "Noted Grave Robber Dead." August 29, 1904.
Sheridan (IN) News. "Lucius R. Stout Accused." December 19, 1902.
South Bend (IN) Tribune. "Take Gang of Ghouls." September 29, 1902.
Star Press (Muncie, IN). "Alexander Is Guarded in His Home." February 14, 1903.
———. "Ghoul King on Stage." August 16, 1910.
———. "His Father's Body Stolen by the Man he Convicted." July 18, 1903.
———. "King of the Ghouls and Aid Sentenced." February 6, 1916.
———. "Robber of Graves to Have Freedom." May 1, 1909.
Western Kansas World (WaKeeney, KS). "Could Not Reach a Verdict." February 28, 1903.

THE GREAT SCHOOL CONTROVERSY

Indianapolis News. "3rd Parties Enter Carmel-Fishers School Battles." September 7, 1954.

Indianapolis Star. "Three Hamilton Townships Unite School Districts." December 17, 1953.
———. "Two Hamilton Consolidation Tickets Lose." November 4, 1954.
Noblesville Ledger. "Advisory Board Refuses to Sign Delaware Budget." September 14, 1954.
———. "All Eyes Focused on School Battle; Quiet Elsewhere." October 30, 1954.
———. "Begin Circulating Petitions Calling for Twp. Change." July 13, 1954.
———. "City and County Items." November 3, 1869.
———. "Clay-Delaware Twp. Division Approved." August 1, 1955
———. "Co Commissioners Meet to Consider What to Do with Township Revision Proposal." February 27, 1952.
———. "County Commissioners." June 11, 1875.
———. "Delaware Twp. Features Famous Connor Settlement." June 29, 1973.
———. "Designed to Aid Situation in 3 South Townships." February 23, 1955.
———. "Election Next Tuesday." August 19, 1913.
———. "Eller Buys Seven Lots, Seeks Five Additional Acres." July 20, 1955.
———. "Favors School Consolidation." October 28, 1954.
———. "Looking Backward." August 23, 1935.
———. "Measure Enables Delaware to Split at White River." March 8, 1955.
———. "46 Freeholders in Fall Creek Tp. Ask Withdraw Names." February 25, 1952.
———. "New Party Files Official Papers." August 12, 1954.
———. "Proponents Move Case Dismissal by Appellate Court." December 3, 1953.
———. "Proposal to Consolidate 2 Townships." November 28, 1945.
———. "The Proposed Consolidation." August 20, 1913.
———. "School Board Organized at Carmel." May 19, 1947.
———. "School Consolidation Rejected by Voters." November 3, 1954.
———. "School Controversy Brings Out Another New Political Party." September 1, 1954.
———. "They Are Not Vigilantes." September 18, 1954.
———. "The Township Question." March 19, 1875.
———. "Township Case Set for Trial on November 10." September 12, 1952.
———. "What Next." July 3, 1956.

Sheridan (IN) News. "Will Case Is Still Grinding." April 26, 1912.
Shirts, Augustus Finch. *A History of Hamilton County, Indiana*. Salem, MA: Higginson Book Company, 1901.

THE MYSTERIOUS TRITTIPO BOMBINGS

Bristol (IN) Banner. "Indiana State News." January 29, 1892.
Fishers Council Minutes. May 17, 1889.
———. July 2, 1892.
———. July 22, 1912
———. August 4, 1914.
Hamilton County Democrat. "Birds Escape." November 17, 1893.
———. "Condensed News of Hamilton County." December 20, 1901.
———. "A Death Trap." January 29, 1892.
———. "The Democrat." June 1, 1900.
———. "The End Not Yet." January 29, 1892.
———. "Fishers Station." March 18, 1887.
———. "Infernal Machine." June 21, 1895.
———. "New Britton." June 9, 1882.
———. "New Cases Filed." August 26, 1892.
———. "Samuel Trittipo Dead." April 10, 1903.
———. "Saturday's News." December 16, 1887.
———. "Trouble at Fishers." March 4, 1892.
Hamilton County Ledger. "Circuit Court." December 2, 1892.
———. "Father Against Son." April 14, 1899.
———. "Fishers Station—Anarchist at Work." January 29, 1892.
———. "Fuzee in Trouble." October 14, 1898.
———. "The Ledger." March 16, 1900.
———. "Plead Guilty." May 13, 1898.
———. "A Saloon Fight." April 8, 1898.
Heighway, David. "Early Fishers—The Trittipo Bombings." https://www.hepl.lib.in.us/early-fishers-the-trittipo-bombings.
Indianapolis News. "Indiana Postmasters Appointed." April 28, 1893.
Noblesville Ledger. "Fifty Years Ago." April 15, 1936.
Star Press (Muncie, IN). "Is Blown Up by Dynamite." May 22, 1914.
St. Louis (MO) Globe-Democrat. "Special Dispatch." June 15, 1895.

Turkey Shoot Leads to Murder

Cicero Gazette (Noblesville, IN). "Noblesville Locals." March 9, 1876.
Daily News-Democrat (Huntington, IN). "The Old Custom Is Fading Away." November 23, 1904.
Hamilton County Ledger. "Educational Items." January 28, 1898.
———. "The Independent." October 16, 1880.
———. "An Old Crime Recalled." April 16, 1897.
Indianapolis News. "City News." February 19, 1878.
———. "Murder." December 27, 1875.
Indiana State Sentinel. "The Republican Convention." February 23, 1876.
Ledger (Noblesville, IN). "Farmers." April 17, 1885.
Logansport (IN) Pharos-Tribune. "Thanksgiving Turkey." November 21, 1896.
Noblesville Ledger. "Affray at a Shooting Match." December 31, 1875.
———. "Carmel Legion Thanksgiving Turkey Shoot." November 20, 1936.
———. "Constables." October 23, 1874.
———. "Dr. Loehr Answers Death Summons." March 29, 1920.
———. "James Redwine." December 31, 1875.
———. "The Little Pistol." March 12, 1875.
———. "Why Is It?" January 7, 1876.
Princeton (IN) Clarion-Leader. "Obituary—Major J.W. Gordon." May 5, 1887.

Robbery of the Fishers National Bank

Courier-Journal (Louisville, KY). "Bank Holdup Suspects Held to Grand Jury." July 14, 1937.
———. "Does Crime Pay?" August 28, 1948.
Edinburg (IN) Daily Courier. "Ferguson Arrested in Connection with Theft at Noblesville." March 31, 1930.
———. "Wilbur Ferguson Found Dead." April 3, 1953.
Evening Star (Franklin, IN). "Celebrated the Fourth." July 7, 1913.
Federal Deposit Insurance Corporation. "Who Is the FDIC?" https://www.fdic.gov/about/learn/symbol/.
Franklin (IN) Evening Star. "Three Arrests Made Wednesday by Sheriff." June 5, 1929.
Indianapolis News. "Alleged Bank Bandit's Trial Set for March 24." March 15, 1930.

Indianapolis Star. "Escaped Prisoner Obtains Parole, Reports for Draft." August 24, 1944.
———. "Four Men Confess Holdup of Bank after Police Quiz." October 31, 1926.
———. "Quick on the Trigger." December 7, 1920.
———. "Restaurant Row Leads to Arrest of Wanted Man." February 26, 1930.
———. "Ryan Bank Robbery Hearing Is Delayed." March 24, 1930.
———. "Third Suspect in Fishers Bank Robbery Is Captured." April 6, 1930.
Interior Journal (Stanford, KY). "Dunnville Bank Robbed: Two of Three Robbers Held in Jail." June 22, 1937.
———. "Dunnville Bank Robbers Given Sentences." October 15, 1937.
Journal and Courier (Lafayette, IN). "Arrest of Six Men Breaks up Robbery Ring." September 20, 1922.
———. "2 Bandits Loot State National Bank of $12,000." February 24, 1930.
Messenger (Madisonville, KY). "One of Three Robbers Held." June 18, 1937.
Muncie (IN) Evening Press. "Trio Holds Up Fishers Bank." February 24, 1930.
Noblesville Ledger. "Alleged Bank Bandit Said to be Part Indian." March 4, 1930.
———. "Bank Cashier Resigns." April 6, 1923.
———. "Bank Robber Paroled From State Prison." September 4, 1936.
———. "Bonds from the Fishers Bank Found on Ryan." February 27, 1930.
———. "Butz Identified with Local Bank." March 31, 1930.
———. "Clearing Decks to Try Alleged Bank Bandit." March 20, 1930.
———. "Court Holds Stolen Bonds Must Be Paid." October 17, 1935.
———. "Escape Local Bank Robber from Prison." August 8, 1936.
———. "Fishers Bank Bandit Will Leave Prison." May 25, 1935.
———. "Fishers Has a Real Boom in Business." December 17, 1934.
———. "Fishers National Bank." December 16, 1925.
———. "Money Secured From Bank on Forged Paper Recovered." July 1, 1915.
———. "Nine Boarders at the Local Jail." March 18, 1930.
———. "Notice." February 26, 1920.
———. "Old Man Pope Sentenced." July 7, 1915.
———. "Ready for Business." May 7, 1920.
———. "Recovery of Bonds Stolen from Bank." April 4, 1930.

———. "Ryan in Court Again for his Sentence." March 29, 1930.
———. "Sound Financial Institution." July 4, 1919.
———. "Stolen Bonds Still Missing." August 5, 1931.
———. "Suspect Is Held in Robbery of Fishers Bank." February 26, 1930.
———. "Two More Fishers Gang of Bandits Are in Custody." April 18, 1930.
Office of the Comptroller of the Currency. "History: 150 Years of the OCC." https://www.occ.treas.gov/about/what-we-do/history/index-history.html,
Republic (Columbus, IN). "Bank Robberies Sweep Midwest." September 19, 1930.
———. "Edinburg Man Admits Part in Bank Hold-up." April 3, 1930.
———. "Gets Term for Fishers Holdup." April 9, 1930.
———. "Two Sentenced in Robbery Case." March 17, 1923.
Star Press (Muncie, IN). "Hamilton County Bank Bandits Get $10,000." February 25, 1930.
Tribune (Seymour, IN). "Guard Noblesville Jail to Avert Ryan Delivery." March 15, 1930.

THE MURDER OF CONSTABLE FRANK CAREY

Buffalo (NY) Weekly Express. "Cyclone Johnson Killed." June 14, 1900.
Courier (Waterloo, IA). "His Slayer Is Unknown." June 15, 1900.
Fadley, James P. *Thomas Taggart: Public Servant, Political Boss: 1856–1929.* Indianapolis: Indiana Historical Society, 1997.
Hamilton County (IN) Ledger. "Big Public Sale." August 17, 1900.
———. "Clay Township Mass Convention." February 26, 1892.
———. "Double Murder." June 12, 1900.
———. "Frank Carey's Obituary." June 15, 1900.
———. "School History." Aug 7, 1903.
Hancock (IN) Democrat. "Two Shot to Death." June 21, 1900.
Indiana Digital Archives. "David W. Patty." http://secure.in.gov/apps/iara/search/Home/Detail?rId=1180837.
Indianapolis Journal. "The Carmel Killing." June 10, 1900.
———. "Johnson's Record Here." June 9, 1900.
———. "Jury Reaches a Verdict." November 25, 1899.
Shirts, Augustus. *History of Hamilton County, Indiana*. Salem, MA: Higginson Book Company, 1901.

THE PHARMACIST WHO SOLD MORE THAN DRUGS

Enterprise (Noblesville, IN). "The Blind Tiger Law." February 15, 1907.

———. "Blind Tiger Law." May 17, 1907.

———. "Six to Six." February 14, 1908.

Hamilton County Ledger. "Druggist in Trouble." January 11, 1907.

———. "Franklin Found Guilty." June 7, 1907.

———. "Harrison Divorce Case." September 29, 1908.

———. "Harrison Gave Bond." January 15, 1907.

———. "Jail Notes." January 18, 1907.

———. "Peruna, Not Whiskey." February 11, 1908.

———. "Senate Bills." March 22, 1907.

———. "Taken to Jail by Prosecutor." January 11, 1907.

Hedeen, Jane. "The Road to Prohibition in Indiana." Indiana Historical Society. https://www.indianahistory.org/wp-content/uploads/1d7d71dfbb39529a736fdba5279a5ba9.pdf.

Noblesville Ledger. "Fishers: 'Collection of Friendly Neighbors.'" September 29, 1988.

Sullivan, Jack. "The Peruna Story: Strumming That Old Catarrh." May 2007. https://www.fohbc.org/PDF_Files/Peruna_JSullivan.pdf.

ABOUT THE AUTHOR

Robert Bowling is a retired police officer with twenty years of experience. He was employed by the Durham (NC) and Fishers (IN) Police Departments. Before retiring from the Fishers Police Department, in addition to his many other duties, he was the department historian and curator. He has received grants through the Indiana Historical Society to further the mission of preserving the department's history.

He currently serves as vice-president of the Historic Ambassador House and Heritage Gardens located in Fishers. He is a board member and historian for the Fishers Historical Society. He is also an active member of the Theodore Roosevelt Association along with its Indiana chapter.

He currently writes historical articles for the local newspaper, *Current in Fishers*. He also organized a historical reenactment of the Battle of Mudsock, featured in this book. He wrote the script for the play and acted. He now teaches criminal justice to high school students and continues to be active with historical organizations. He lives in Fishers with his family.